THE BIBLE NOW!

THE BIBLE NOW!

Joseph A. Grispino

FIDES PUBLISHERS, INC.
NOTRE DAME, INDIANA

LCCCN: 73-175427

ISBN: 0-8190-0399-9

To M. Saunders

Foreword

From 1960 to 1969 the author has been engaged in popularizing biblical scholarship in his quarterly, *Current Scripture Notes*. The French would label this genre of popularization, *"haute vulgarization."*

The present book contains seven articles which appeared in *Current Scripture Notes* but they have been rewritten for this publication. Three chapters—"Does the Devil Exist?," "Did Jesus Christ Found A Church?," and "Is Jesus Christ God?"—have never been previously published.

Usually readers are exhorted to keep up-to-date on biblical interpretations because of the advances in archaeology, history and philology. This book would like to offer an exhortation on a different key. The key is simply this. This modest book attempts to exhort readers to keep abreast of biblical interpretations due to the advances in the century old hassle of biblical inerrancy. Accordingly, the first chapter, "Biblical Inerrancy," is intended to give a solid foundation to readers concerning the problem of error in the Bible. All the following chapters, consequently, are examples of how novel biblical theories may be read in the light of the final explanation of inerrancy as offered by Vatican II.

The articles have been selected because they are topical and hence the title, *The Bible Now!* Many Catholics, and others, have asked where the Church stands now in the present stage of scientific development on such issues as the existence of angels, devils, hell, original sin, the Church, the hierarchy, remarriage, Christ's resurrection and divinity. If some Catholics feel uncomfortable about what they would call the liberal views expressed within these pages, they may find some comfort in the fact that all these views are found embedded in learned and foreign Catholic journals.

May the articles not only help to keep the educated layman and busy cleric up-to-date, but may they also be used for class discussion on the upper high school and college levels.

The biblical quotations are from *The New American Bible*.

San Fernando Valley State College JOSEPH A. GRISPINO
California
March 1971

Contents

I

Biblical Inerrancy

Throughout the history of Christianity one of the biggest problems for Christian scholars has been the interpretation of Scripture. Part of the problem has centered around the belief in biblical inerrancy, that is, the belief that the Bible can contain no error. This is a simple enough belief, but its explanation is by no means so simple, especially in the face of the inescapable fact that the Bible *does, or at least appears to,* contain error. But after centuries of scholarly debate on the issue, a breakthrough came at last in the Dogmatic Constitution on Divine Revelation of Vatican II, which takes a positive stand on the question of error in the Bible. Up to the time of this Constitution (November 18, 1965) official Church documents on the Bible had always expressed the negative effect of the inspiration of the Bible, namely, freedom from error or inerrancy. (In fact, the first two drafts of the Dogmatic Constitution on Divine Revelation followed this tradition. Only in the third draft came the dramatic breakthrough.)

The present writer has seen hardly any popular Catholic articles in English on the subject. Few commentaries

1

on the Dogmatic Constitution mention the breakthrough and those that do have not elaborated upon it. It is unfortunate that we still find ourselves explaining biblical inerrancy. The cherished hope of many Catholic biblical scholars is that the issue be phased out of biblical studies. But this phasing out cannot be accomplished through silence, for there are too many Catholics who are not scholars who would continue in confusion, having been taught at some point in their lives that the Bible cannot be wrong.

We will discuss below the problem of biblical inerrancy before Vatican II, then the text of the Dogmatic Constitution on Divine Revelation, finally some of the types of errors in the Bible.

The Problem Of Inerrancy before Vatican II

The long-standing view on biblical inerrancy asserted simply that the Bible does not teach error. As early as the second century, the era of the Fathers of the Church, this view was simply accepted without much critical understanding. Not until the nineteenth century, with the flourishing of the natural sciences, archaeology, and historiography, did statements in the Bible begin to be examined critically.

As new discoveries in the nineteenth and early twentieth centuries nurtured critical attitudes toward the Bible, Christian apologists tried to safeguard the truth in the Bible as they saw it by adopting the system called concordism. This was an attempt to explain the Bible by showing that it agreed with the newest discoveries of science. For example, in the Genesis account of the creation of the world, the six days were interpreted as agreeing with the geological periods of the formation of the world. But this artificial system was too weak to endure. Meanwhile, historians and archaeologists, often with gleeful cynicism, pointed to one biblical error after another in matters of history, chronology, geography, and the natural sciences.

Catholic scholars reacted to these disturbing discoveries by trying to limit the possibility of biblical errors in various ways. A full account of these ways is not important for our purposes here—we will give just two illustrations. Cardinal Newman suggested removal of the "obiter dicta" ("insignificant sayings") from biblical inerrancy. For him the inspired writer's offhand remark about Tobit's dog wagging its tail could be a mistake because it was something said merely in the course of the narrative and unimportant for the truth of the whole passage.

A more serious suggestion came from the French scholars, such as d'Hulst and Loisy, who proposed that the Bible could be wrong in matters pertaining to the natural sciences, to history, or to anything *except* faith and morals.

The weakness of these and similar attempts to justify the "truth" of the Bible lay in limiting the possible erroneous material in the Bible to definite sections of the Bible. Theoretically, for example, much of the Books of Kings could be wrong historically because this material did not deal with matters of faith and/or morals.

This theory of "material limitation" never satisfied serious scholars. It clearly implied or supposed that there were parts of the Bible that were not inspired by God. The principal refutation against the theory of material limitation was that the entire Bible was inspired because as a whole it refers to God's plan of salvation. The artificial material distinction was refused acceptance by Popes Leo XIII, Pius X, and finally by Pius XII in his encyclical of 1943, *Divino Afflante Spiritu.*

The Study of Literary Forms

Divino Afflante Spiritu gave great impetus to the revival of biblical scholarship by giving the "green light" to research by Catholic biblical scholars. The area of research particularly encouraged by the encyclical was the application of the study of oriental literary forms to the Bible. In this regard, the encyclical stated:

> The interpreter must . . . accurately determine what modes of writing . . . the authors of that ancient period would be likely to use, and in fact did use. . . . What those exactly were the commentator cannot determine as it were in advance, but only after a careful examination of the ancient literature of the East. . . . By this knowledge and exact appreciation of the modes of speaking and writing in use among the ancients can be solved many difficulties, which are raised against the veracity and historical value of the Divine Scriptures. . . .[1]

The study of literary forms helped immensely toward a clarification of inerrancy. It untied many of the knotty problems and focused attention on how literature communicates truth. Literary forms are used by everyone who communicates through language. Whenever we write, we employ a particular literary form or type of lit-

---

1. St. Meinrad, *Rome and the Study of Scripture,* 1958 ed., Para. 35, 36, 39.

erature. The daily newspaper contains examples of many types of literary forms: news articles, editorials, book reviews, letters to the editor, serialized short stories, poems, comics, political cartoons, advertisements. Each of these forms of literature has its own form of expression. We know, as we go from one form to another, that "each literary form has its own truth." The editorials, for instance, are to be understood much more literally than the short stories, poems, advertisements, and comics.

The various books of the Bible must also be interpreted each according to its own form of literature. Since God chose to speak to men through men, He used the manner of communication of men. But men use a variety of literary forms in writing. Therefore, the only way we have of understanding God's message for us is through the correct understanding and identification of the literary forms used by the inspired writers. Consequently, each biblical book must be interpreted according to its literary form. If this rule is carried out, very many problems with the belief of inerrancy disappear. A difficulty that arises is that it is hard to interpret the many literary forms in the Bible that are ancient, Eastern and foreign to Westerners of the twentieth century. A few examples will bear this out.

Examples of Literary Forms in the Bible

If the two Genesis accounts of creation are read as though they were a modern scientific account of the creation of the world, then the reader is bound to find "errors," such as the picture of the world as a disk floating above the waters. But if we read these two accounts according to the literary form the author intended and as he was understood by his readers, we will see that he was writing a type of *religious* history. He was teaching one lesson—that God made everything! He dressed up this skeletal message in the myth acceptable to the prescientific people of his era.

The Book of Judith, if interpreted as strict history instead of the fictionalized history that it is, is found to contain many historical and geographical errors. Nebuchadnezzar, for instance, is called king of the Assyrians when historically he was king of the neo-Babylonians and began to reign about eight years after the Assyrian empire collapsed.

The first Book of Maccabees uses another unfamiliar literary form. Although the author does not write like a modern historian, his book contains generally historical truth, with chronological and topographical precision. Yet, he writes "propagandist history." The propaganda favors the Maccabean dynasty because the Maccabees fought for and preached the observance of the Mosaic Law and the traditional customs. The Jewish revolt against Greek culture is pictured as a world-shattering event. All opposition to the Jewish way of life is blanketed under "children of the devil." The author puts speeches on the lips of Judas Maccabees and his brother Jonathan which extol the legitimacy and necessity of the revolution. The numbers of enemy soldiers are exaggerated to enhance the heroism of the divinely protected Maccabean armies whose victories are exaggerated and whose defeats are minimized.

The literary form of the first part of the Book of Daniel (ch. 1-6) is one of the most disconcerting in the Old Testament for modern readers. This form is called *"hagga-*

doth," i.e. edifying religious stories. These may be compared to the stories of the Christian martyrs. Such stories were common in the Hellenistic world. The author of such a story enshrines an edifying lesson within an interesting folklore setting.

In passing over into the New Testament, we notice that some parts of the Gospels are written according to a literary form whose model has not yet been found in all the literature of antiquity. The most peculiar feature is that the Gospels may be read on three different levels. The first and most obvious is the "situation in the life of Jesus." This is the historical level—the actual words and deeds of the Lord. The second level is that of the "situation in the Gospel." This refers to the manner and purpose of the evangelist in arranging his Gospel the way he did. This level is also called "redactional history," the history of Gospel composition. An illustration is Matthew's account of the "Sermon on the Mount," in which parts of many different talks given by Jesus were combined. The third level is the "life-situation of the early church." The second part of the parable of the sower (Mt. 13:18-23) is an appropriate example of this level. In this passage the explanation of the parable is not actually the words of Jesus, but is rather the evangelist's adaptation of the parable to the problems or "situation" of the early Church for whom he was writing.

The Dogmatic Constitution on Revelation

The earlier, noncritical view of biblical inerrancy which taught that the Bible contained no error was based upon the following line of reasoning: God is the author of the

Bible; God cannot be the author of error; therefore, the Bible can contain no error. This is logical reasoning, but it is grossly oversimplified; and it simply cannot explain the actual and obvious presence of errors in the Bible. The study of literary forms has shed much light upon difficult areas of the Bible, but there remain difficult passages not explained by literary forms. This brings us to the breakthrough of Vatican II.

The Dogmatic Constitution on Divine Revelation states that the truth contained in Scripture is essentially directed to the salvation of men: ". . . The books of Scripture must be acknowledged as teaching firmly, faithfully, and without error that truth which God wanted put into the sacred writings for the sake of our salvation."[2] This means that the truth which must be sought in the Bible is the truth *which brings men to salvation,* that is, the salvific truth, and not the truths of natural sciences and secular history.

The previous draft of the Constitution had read: "The books of Scripture must be acknowledged as teaching firmly, faithfully, and without error that *salutary* truth which God wanted put into the sacred writings." (Italics mine.) The phrase "salutary truth" could have resulted in again placing material limitations on possible erring sections in the Bible—separating inerrant parts (those pertaining to faith and morals, "salutary,") from possible errant parts (e.g. those pertaining to history and natural sciences.) To obviate the material-limitation of biblical inerrancy the third and present draft was decided upon:

---

2. W. M. Abbott, *The Documents of Vatican II,* Gen. Ed., Guild Press, 1966, ch. 3, no. 11, p. 119.

"That truth . . . for the sake of our salvation." This final expression conveys the dynamic nature of inspired biblical truth; i.e., biblical truth plays a positive role in saving men insofar as its main purpose is to teach how God presents himself as a friend, inviting men to faith in him and to salvation.

In summary, we may say that according to the teaching of Vatican II, the Bible contains *the* truth, i.e., God's plan for man's salvation. This truth of the Bible must be understood as a progressive revelation of God's salvific plan from Old Testament beginnings until the plan was finally realized in Christ's words and deeds. The truth of each text or section of the Bible must be understood within the framework of the whole of biblical revelation and its progressive character. No truth is revealed except in connection with the general truth and purpose of salvation history. *This is the sense in which the Bible is free from error.*

Factual Errors in the Bible

The Dogmatic Constitution indicates two principles to solve the problem of scriptural inerrancy, namely, the principle of literary forms, and the "theological" principle that the main truth taught by the Bible is "that truth . . . for the sake of our salvation." The theological principle is necessary because the principle of literary forms does not explain some of the factual errors in the Bible. Let us test this principle with two examples.

The first example is from the Gospel of Matthew, in which it is stated that the death of Judas verified the prophecy of Jeremiah. The prophecy concerned was actually made by Zechariah. Matthew 27:9, 10, reads: "Then what was spoken through Jeremiah the prophet was fulfilled, 'They took the thirty silver pieces, the price set on a man's head (for that was his price among the Israelites), and gave money for the potter's field, as the Lord directed me.' " In reality this is a free quotation from Zechariah 11:12-13: "I said to them, 'If it seems good to you, give me my wages; but if not, let it go.' And they counted out my wages, thirty pieces of silver. But the Lord said to me, 'Throw it in the treasury, the handsome price at which they valued me.' So I took the thirty pieces of silver and threw them into the treasury in the house of the Lord."

The second example is from Mark 2:26, which states that "Abiathar" was the high priest when David ate the consecrated loaves. Actually the high priest, or the priest, was Achimelech, his father, as we know from 1 Samuel 21:1-7: ". . . and David said to Achimelech the priest . . . 'Now what have you on hand? Give me five loaves, or whatever you can find.' But the priest replied to David, 'I have no ordinary bread on hand, only holy bread'; . . . So the priest gave him holy bread, for no other bread was on hand. . . ."

Until the time of Vatican II these factual errors were very embarrassing to Catholic scholars, especially when they could not be explained as resulting from a particular literary form. There is no doubt that there are many literary forms in the Bible which do allow factual error, for example, the religious historical writings of the Books of Judith, Esther, etc. But the literary forms of the Gospel in these two sections of Matthew and Mark do not allow for factual errors even if we admit that the evangelists' main assertion of truth was not concerned with these two incidentals but with something more important. Hence another aspect in the study of biblical inerrancy is that we can simply admit the presence of factual errors in the Bible.

Errors in Religious Matters

So far we have been speaking of so-called errors in matters pertaining to natural sciences and history in the Bible. We have shown that these are not really errors if we properly understand the literary forms in which these alleged errors are embedded. Moreover, we have shown that there are some real factual errors in the Bible which cannot be explained away by literary form. Let us test the theological principle of Vatican II further by asking whether we may admit that at times an inspired writer made a genuine mistake in a matter pertaining to religious belief.

In principle, it seems that we may answer affirmatively. Even if there is a mistaken religious notion here and there in the Bible, this does not negate the theological principle that primarily the Bible teaches the one religious truth of salvation. The Bible as a whole conveys this truth even if there are found some errors in religious teachings in the Bible.

As an example of how the above principle helps us to solve problems resulting from the presence of apparent errors in religious belief, we will cite a controversy between two biblical scholars in the early part of the twentieth century. The dispute between two Jesuits, Fathers Drum and Lattey, centered on whether or not Paul believed that he would be alive at the end of the world, at Jesus' second coming (the *parousia*). The text in question was 1 Thessalonians 4:15-17: ". . . We who live, who survive until his coming, will in no way have an advantage over those who have fallen asleep. . . . Those who have died in Christ will rise first. Then we, the living, the survivors, will be caught up with them in the clouds to meet the Lord in the air. Thenceforth we shall be with the Lord unceasingly." The Thessalonians were worried about whether they and their dear ones who had passed away would rise again. Paul explains to them that first Jesus will come at the end of the world, then the dead Christians will rise, and finally those *living* at the end of the world will go to heaven with the risen Christians. Therefore the Thessalonians should not mourn but "comfort one another with these words" because death for them is really different from that of the pagans who do not have the hope of the resurrection.

The most obvious meaning of this passage is that Paul expected to be alive at the second coming of Jesus. This is a common interpretation found in scholarly Protestant commentaries, which often say outright that Paul erred. But since the Church was still bound to the denial of error in the Bible, Father Lattey proposed that Paul erred in his private opinion only, i.e. that he was not *teaching* this as fact. Father Drum asserted that Paul did not err in either a private or a public opinion, but that he *hoped*— not taught—that he would live until the parousia. With arguments from Greek syntax, Drum showed that it could not be proven that Paul was including himself with those living at the end of the world and that the "we who live, who survive" merely meant the general "we" of those, whoever they might be, who would be alive at the end of the world. In using this general "we," Paul did not necessarily include himself. Rome's pontifical biblical commission finally, on June 18, 1915, decided in favor of Father Drum's interpretation that Paul did not err either privately or publicly.

It is doubtful that these learned arguments would have been necessary had it not been for the Church's strict stand on biblical inerrancy. Granted that the victorious scholar's position may still be well argued, it seems equally tenable to hold with modern Protestant commentators that Paul erred. (Only later in life did Paul realize that he would not live till the second coming of Jesus.) The essential truth—"that truth for the sake of our salvation"—contained in the cited passage is that Jesus will save and raise men at his final coming. This remains true even if Paul erred in believing that he would be alive to witness this event.

Another example of a religious error is found in the Book of Job, ch. 14:7-22, in which the author denies the existence of an afterlife: "But when a man dies, all vigor leaves him; when man expires, where then is he? As when the waters of a lake fail, or a stream grows dry and parches, so men lie down and rise not again. Till the heavens are no more, they shall not awake, nor be roused out of their sleep" (verses 10-12). This seems a direct contradiction to the words of Jesus in Matthew 25:46: "And these (the damned) will go off to eternal punishment and the just to eternal life."

How can we explain this obvious contradiction in the light of Vatican II? Some authors reply that the author of Job did not make an error but that he only wrote an incomplete truth. The truth was completed in Mt. 25:46. This explanation is based on the teaching that there is only one author of the whole Bible, namely, the Holy Spirit. Thus if a human author of the Bible makes an error in a religious matter the Holy Spirit completes or rectifies the error in a later biblical writing.

How reasonable is such an explanation of a religious error? Theologically, the appeal to the one author of the Bible, the Holy Spirit, is correct. However, if we simply admit that the biblical author of Job made an error, this does not militate against the one central truth of the Bible that God saves all men. If one objects that Job did not err because no one at that time knew of the afterlife, then we would reply that therefore we cannot accuse medieval man of error in his belief that the world was flat because at that time no one knew that it was round. It is more honest to say that just as we would accuse the medieval or ancient man of error in saying that the world was flat, so we must admit the error of these biblical authors in denying the afterlife.

In summary and conclusion, any apparent error in the Bible may be answered by an appeal to the literary principle of literary forms; any real error may be answered by an appeal to the positive theological principle of biblical truth embodied in the Dogmatic Constitution on Divine Revelation.

II

Do Angels Exist?

While the existence of angels may not be a problem of central importance to theology, for centuries there have been many popular beliefs surrounding the angels and for this reason we will take up the question. In recent years educated Christians have become increasingly skeptical about the existence of angels. Confusion about the issue is intensified when the popular press makes such statements as: "Many contemporary Christian theologians concede the mythic character of most religious references to angels."[1]

In this chapter we will consider the biblical data on angels and how we are to interpret the data, and what dogmatic theologians say about this biblical material.[2]

Angels in the Old Testament

The English word *angel* comes from the Latin word *angelus* which is a transcription of *angelos* in Greek. An-

---

1. *Time,* 10-6-67, p. 58.
2. We do not intend to discuss the *philosophical* arguments for the existence of angels, though philosophy may offer plausible arguments for the existence of such beings.

gelos is used in the Greek translation of the Old Testament (the Septuagint) to translate the Hebrew word *mal'ak,* usually rendered "messenger." The Old Testament uses other expressions for angels such as "sons of God," "the host of the Lord," "the host of heaven," and "the holy ones."

The Old Testament describes the angels appearing as human males (without wings). For example, in the story of Jacob's vision at Bethel, angels ascended and descended on a ladder from heaven (cf. Gn. 28:10-15). The angels are considered to be attendants at God's heavenly court. They praise him and are sent as messengers to men. The Hebrew word for angel, *mal'ak,* connotes this function of messenger—not necessarily a personal messenger, but any divine presence or effective expression of God's power. The personal aspect of this messenger comes more from the Greek translation *angelos* and from late theological speculation than from the Old Testament. The Old Testament Hebrews did not try to describe the nature of angels—they did not give this much thought; they simply thought of angels as belonging to heaven and as different from men, even though they were *pictured* in human form. It follows, then, that "angel" in the Old Testament does not mean "separated spiritual substance" as modern theologians use the term. The Bible does not speak of angels as "substance" nor as "spiritual." The angels are not called "spirits."[3] The biblical notion of

---

3. This is true even in the disputed Psalm 103:4: "Yahweh makes his angels [mal'akim, plural of *mal'ak*] into winds" (not into "spirits" as some translations have it).

"spirit" (*ruah* in Hebrew) is different from "messenger."
Ruah means wind, breath of life, spirit.

Besides the "ordinary" angels in the Old Testament,
there are two special groups of superhuman beings called
Cherubim and Seraphim, which have been classed as
angels in popular thought, though the Old Testament
never calls them such. No description is given of the
Cherubim standing on guard at the tree of life in the story
of Adam and Eve's exile from Eden (Gn.3 :24). However,
archaeologists believe that they should be visualized in
human form like the contemporary Babylonian "karibi"
who, with a sword of jagged flames, guarded the en-
trances of the temples. The Cherubim over the ark of the
covenant in the Holy of Holies of King Solomon's temple
were each made with two outstretched wings and were
probably sculptured in human form. The Cherubim
which were woven into the curtains and veil of the taber-
nacle and which decorated the paneling and doors of
Solomon's temple and also the Cherubim decorating the
basins of the temple are probably to be visualized in human form, but they may well have had the form of lions
or winged bulls with human faces as suggested by contemporary relief friezes on the walls of Assyrian palaces.
On Ezekiel's chariot the Cherubim have human appearances, yet each one has four faces: the face of a man, of
a lion, of a bull and of an eagle. Each has four wings and
human hands under the wings and four straight legs with
bulls' hooves (Ez. 1:5-8). Similar Cherubim are found
sculptured in Mesopotamian palaces.

The other group of superhuman beings, called the
Seraphim, are mentioned only once in the Old Testament

(Isaiah 6:2-6). They are described as having hands, feet, a human voice and three pairs of wings. With one pair they veil their faces, with another they cover their bodies and feet, with the third, they fly.

The Angel of Yahweh

The earliest example of the belief in angels in the Old Testament seems to be the belief in the "angel of Yahweh" or the angel of God. This angel stops Abraham from sacrificing Isaac (Gn. 22:11); he "wrestles" with Jacob in a dream (Gn. 32:25ff); he appears to Moses at the burning bush (Ex. 3); he leads the Israelites through the Red Sea and desert (Ex. 3:21-22); he appears to Samson's mother (Judges 13:3); he slaughters the Assyrians at Jerusalem (2 Kings 19:35). From these and similar passages it is not always clear whether the angel of Yahweh (*mal'ak* Yahweh) always signifies the same angel. Nevertheless, he is almost always described as prudent and helpful to men. Only once does he punish the Israelites for their faults (2 Sm. 24:16).

In some passages the angel of Yahweh or of God speaks or acts as if he were God himself. For example, the angel of Yahweh called Abraham from heaven, saying: "Do not lay a hand on the boy . . . I know now that you fear *God,* since you have not withheld your only son from *me*" (Gn. 22:11-12). On the other hand, other passages show a more pronounced distinction between Yahweh and the angel of Yahweh. For instance, Yahweh says to the Israelites: "I will send an angel before you, and he will drive out the Canaanites . . . but I myself will not go up with you" (Ex. 33:2-3).

The best explanation of these and similar passages advocates the identity of Yahweh and his angel. The angel of Yahweh or of God is the sensible manifestation, in a metaphorical sense, of the invisible God. This is why in the older biblical passages the angel of Yahweh speaks as if he were God. (See the first example cited above.) Consequently, many scholars explain that at first the expression "the angel of Yahweh" was used to distinguish the person of God from some of his activities, or to avoid making God act in a human manner inconsistent with his supremacy above man. For instance, in the first example above the "angel of the Lord" and not Yahweh himself is said to hold back Abraham's arm. But as the Israelites became more certain of Yahweh's supremacy over nature, the angel of Yahweh was more and more separated from Yahweh and finally became Yahweh's "vizier." (See the second example cited above.)

In conclusion, we may add that the angel of Yahweh is hardly mentioned in the books of the prophets, written from the eighth century onwards. After the sixth century exile the angel is in general clearly distinguished from Yahweh. The angel acts as the messenger, vizier, or executor of God's works. As we shall show further on, the existence of some kind of heavenly beings was simply *accepted* as part of the intellectual world of the sacred writers, and was used by them to teach about God's power, providence, intervention in human affairs and presence in the world. But the fact that there actually exist "separated, spiritual substances" was never *revealed* by God to the sacred writers, and so never actually entered into their *faith,* and was therefore never conveyed to men as an object of *belief.*

Angels in the New Testament

The Gospels, especially the stories of Jesus' infancy, frequently mention angels. The angel Gabriel predicts the birth of John the Baptist and of Jesus, an angel appears to Joseph three times, angels announce Jesus' birth (cf. Luke 1 and 2; Mt. 1 and 2). Angels appear rarely during Jesus' public ministry. They minister to him after his fast in the desert, and an angel strengthens him in the garden of Gethsemani. Angels are always ready to assist him (Mt. 26:53). The angels announce Jesus' resurrection to his disciples and they will accompany him at the end of the world. The angels protect the children and the lowly ones of his kingdom (Mt. 18:10-11).

In the Acts of the Apostles angels continue to be featured in the ministry of the first Christians. An angel frees Peter and John from prison and assists Cornelius, Philip, and Paul.

From this overview we see that the idea of angels in the Gospels and Acts does not proceed beyond the Old Testament idea of the angels.

In his epistles, Paul did not teach anything original as to the different kinds of angels. He merely accepted what was of common Jewish belief. He mentions seven different kinds of angels and superhuman powers throughout his works without intending to number or classify them or specify their different functions. The seven are the "common" angels (Rom. 8:38), archangels (1 Thes. 4:15), thrones (Col. 1:16), dominations, virtues, powers and principalities (Eph. 1:21). The last three are mentioned as evil spirits elsewhere (Rom. 8:38) in the epistles. The last five are never called "angels" by Paul and they may have been taken from the vocabulary of his Jewish opponents.

The traditional number of nine "hierarchical" classes of choirs of angels seems to have been first calculated by St. Ambrose (fourth century) and Pseudo-Dionysius (fifth century). To Paul's seven classes of "angels" there were added the Cherubim and Seraphim of the Old Testament. It is evident that neither tradition in the strict sense nor the Bible speaks of a ninefold hierarchy of angels each with its specific function.

Of much greater significance than his enumeration of the choirs of angels is Paul's teaching that angels are inferior to Jesus and that Jesus alone, and not they, is the one mediator in the new covenant. Paul was attacking false teachers who exaggerated the role of angels (Col. 2:18). Paul took for granted that the angels existed as personal beings but he was not teaching this assumption as part of God's revealed message—he was teaching rather the superiority of Christ over "angels."

The Epistle to the Hebrews gives a great deal of attention to the angels. The main purpose of the Epistle is to show that Jesus' teaching is superior to that of the Old Testament. Probably because of the role which Jewish theology attributed to the angels as messengers of God, the author of Hebrews offers abundant evidence of the inferiority of these angels in rank relative to Jesus. He attempts thereby to prove the inferiority of the revelation of which the angels were the intermediaries. Here again, as in the epistles of Paul, the existence of the angels is presumed, rather than taught as part of God's message.

In the book of Revelation, angels are frequently mentioned. They are not to be interpreted literally but meta-

phorically because according to the literary form of apocalyptic writing, the angels are made the revealers of
God's messages.

Interpretation of the Biblical Data

Having surveyed the biblical roots of the Christian belief in angels, we must consider the meaning of this material. Is the existence of angels in the Bible merely a supposition based on the view of the world and of God held
by the sacred writers? Did the sacred writers merely *assume* the existence of angels as personal beings just as
they presupposed that the earth was flat in their description of God's creation in Genesis? It seems that this is the
case. Just as their prescientific conception of the world
was used as a wrapper to teach the lesson that God made
everything, we may likewise say that the idea of angels
was used as a wrapper to teach such truths as the providence of God or his universal presence.

But what should the writers have said if they had
wanted to say that the existence of angels as personal beings is part of God's message or is "revealed"? They would
certainly have stated more clearly and precisely that angels are personal beings. These writers would have given
more evidence that they were directly concerned with
this problem. If we could find biblical evidence to this
effect, we should have to consider the existence of angels
a revealed doctrine demanding our assent through faith.
But instead, we find that all the biblical texts which mention angels or the angel of Yahweh may be interpreted as
metaphors to express God's providence, or as symbols of
God's presence, activity, attributes and modes of communication with men.

The Church's Teaching on Angels

The traditional view of the Church's teaching on the angels is exemplified in the following statement by J. Michl, a theologian of Munich, Germany, who writes in *New Catholic Encyclopedia,* "Angels," Vol. 1, p. 513:

> The Church has defined as dogma that besides the visible world God also created a kingdom of invisible spirits, called angels, and that he created them before the creation of the world (Lateran Council IV, 1215, ch. 1, Denz 800; repeated at Vatican I, 1870, Denz 3002; cf. earlier, the Nicene Creed of 325, Denz 125 . . .). In conformity with Holy Scripture and the whole of Christian tradition, these angels must be regarded as personal beings and not as mere powers or the like. Pius XII rejected a contrary opinion as being opposed to Catholic doctrine, encyclical *Humani Generis* August 12, 1950, Denz 3891.

This view holds that the doctrine of angels as personal beings is part of God's message—that it is revealed.

There are several objections to this view. First, as we have seen above, a careful reading of the Bible gives insufficient grounds for a clearly expressed doctrine on the angels as personal beings. All that can be reasonably concluded from the biblical data is that the writers *assumed* the existence of the angels. Second, before one can say that the Church has defined as dogma that the angels are personal beings, one must show that that precise statement was directly intended by the Church's definition. But the text of the Fourth Lateran Council (see above for Michl's quotation of the council) does not appear to define the existence of angels as personal beings. Third, to say, as Michl says above, that angels are personal beings "in conformity with . . . the whole Christian tradition" may mean tradition in the sense of a tradition which assumed the existence of angels as personal beings in an uncritical way: therefore, "Christian tradition" does not mean tradition in a strict theological sense. Fourth, the warning of Pope Pius XII must not be insisted upon too much because all that his encyclical says in this regard is: "Some also question whether angels are personal beings." (Moreover, theologians have not yet adequately explained the doctrinal authority of papal encyclicals.)

A view different from the traditional one and more in harmony with what we can deduce from the biblical evidence is the interpretation of Karl Rahner and H. Vorgrimler in their *Theological Dictionary* (1965, p. 21): "The purely spiritual nature of the angels becomes a thesis of angelology (St. Thomas Aquinas) only on the occasion of the Fourth Lateran Council which *presupposes the existence of the angels.* Finally, a recent declaration of the magisterium (*Humani Generis* D. 2318) takes to task those who question the personal character of the angels or the essential differences between spirit and matter . . . . The theological doctrine of the angels must begin with the fact that the original source of doctrine about the angels is not the revelation of God himself, either in the Old Testament or the New Testament; that *in this revelation the angels are merely taken for granted* and their existence experienced, as created, personal, structural principles within the harmony of the cosmic order" (emphasis added). In other words, these two prominent theologians are saying, *Humani Generis* notwithstanding, that since the biblical writers took for granted the existence of angels, they thereby experienced the angels as created personal beings who were considered part of the world structure, as intermediaries between God and man. The presupposition of angels as personal beings in the Bible is the same presupposition underlying all the relevant ecclesiastical documents from the Nicene Creed to *Humani Generis* of 1950. Hence, just as the Bible cannot be used as a proof of the existence of individual angels, neither can these ecclesiastical documents.[4]

Related Problems

Popular belief has made much of the devotion to the "guardian angels." Old Testament examples of such "guardian" angels include Raphael, who accompanied Tobit on his voyage; Michael as the angel of the Israelites or of Judah in the book of Daniel; other angels as national guardians of the Persians (Dn. 10:13) and of Greece (Dn. 10:21).

The clearest example of the notion of guardian angel is found in Mt. 18:10 where Jesus says: "See that you never despise one of these little ones. I assure you, their angels in heaven constantly behold my heavenly Father's face." Here and elsewhere Jesus may very well have been following the Jewish ideas of his day without necessarily meaning to pronounce on the question of whether angels are real personal beings or not.

Thus, the biblical data on guardian angels may be interpreted in the same manner as all the above data on angels in the Old and New Testaments; i.e., the assumption

---

4. K. Rahner seems to have a different view in the article on "Angels" in *Sacramentum Mundi,* Vol. I, wherein he claims that Lateran IV and Vatican I declare dogmatically the existence of angels.

that guardian angels existed was accepted from among the popular ideas of the era by the writers of the Old and New Testaments without this assumption forming a part of their faith in what God had revealed. (Note also that the Church has never insisted that the existence of individual guardian angels is a doctrine of faith.)

Another problem related to the existence of the angels concerns the liturgical texts which speak of angels. Those who were responsible for the composition of liturgical texts which included the mention of angels followed in the footsteps of the biblical writers by holding to the popular acceptance of the personal being of angels. The teaching contained in these liturgical texts concerns what the angels represent, such as God's providence, presence, attributes, and activity among men.

For example, in the new canon of the Mass we read: "Almighty God, we pray that your angels may take this sacrifice to your altar in heaven." This text is simply asking that God accept our sacrifice. Actually, "angel" in this text seems to have been an early term for Christ: it is he who takes our sacrifices to the Father.

Conclusion

We may conclude, then, that the Bible, the ecclesiastical documents and tradition have only adopted the popular assumptions about the personal existence of angels, and have not intended their existence to be part of God's *revealed* message nor part of the object of our faith and belief. All the biblical passages dealing with angels can be explained as metaphors expressing God's providence or as symbols of God's presence, activity, attributes, and modes of communication.

If, then, we ask the question "Do angels exist?" we must make a distinction. If by this question we are asking whether the sacred writers revealed the existence of "separated spiritual substances," then the answer is "no" because the writers were never concerned with such philosophical problems. But if by this question one is asking whether God communicates with men, whether he is present and acts and cares for men, then the answer is "yes," angels do exist, insofar as this notion explains God's action.[5]

---

5. It is evident that the problems of angels is only a part of the larger problem of the distinction between matter and spirit, a problem beyond the scope of this present work.

III

Does the Devil Exist?

The famous French writer Baudelaire once said that the devil's cleverest trick is to convince us that he does not exist. Today many Christians have become skeptical about the existence of a devil and of evil spirts. Rudolph Bultmann wrote: "One cannot use electricity and a radio and have recourse to medicine and modern clinics and yet at the same time believe in a world of spirits and miracles of the New Testament." This biblical scholar's remark finds support in an uncontested observation that the more modern technology permeates an uncivilized or backward area, the less its inhabitants attribute events to evil spirits.

Is the existence of devils, demons, evil spirits simply part of the naive mentality of a bygone era, or is it part of divine revelation demanding the assent of faith? Did the biblical writers merely presuppose the existence of devils or did they intend to reveal this as an object of faith? Before beginning the consideration of these questions we must clarify two points. First, by devils we mean non-human beings of a spiritual nature, endowed with intelligence and free will, having a personal relation to this world and to its inhabitants and capable of purposeful activity. Second, we are not considering whether or not philosophy and human reason favor the existence of devils; rather we are limiting our consideration to the teaching of Scripture and the Church.

Our procedure will be to inquire, first, what does the Bible say about devils? Second, what are the recent interpretations of the biblical data on devils? Third, some conclusions of modern systematic theologians. Fourth, some related problems.

Devils in the Old Testament

When one considers the Old Testament roots of the Christian belief in devils, one cannot help but be impressed with the paucity of Old Testament texts which deal with devils and related concepts. Indeed, such scarcity points up the sophistication of the ancient religion of the Hebrews, for their contemporaries had worlds filled with all sorts of evil spirits who were responsible for all sorts of evils. In observing how sparse are the Old Testament roots of our highly developed Christian doctrine on devils, we will be forced to conclude that this development is not scriptural but comes from postbiblical speculation during the early days of Christianity.

The Old Testament concepts from which this speculation originated are (the) satan, the literary personification of evil, the serpent in the creation story of Genesis, the stories of fallen angels, and a few demons and evil spirits borrowed from pagan mythologies. We will consider below those ideas which most influenced Christian speculation.

Satan

The Old Testament Hebrew word *satan* meant an adversary or an accuser at law—equivalent to a prosecutor or district attorney today. The early Israelites spoke of the "sons of God" as members of Yahweh's "council" which assisted him in ruling the universe. The figure of "sons of God" was sometimes used by the authors of the Old Testament books as a substitute for the activity of Yahweh, whose transcendence above all earthly affairs they wanted to stress—particularly if this activity did not meet the highest moral standards. Thus, these sons of God became "satans" or men's accusers before the judgment of Yahweh. There are several examples of this development. Probably the oldest such text is Zechariah 3:1, written around 520-518 B.C.: "Then he showed me Joshua the high priest standing before the angel of the Lord, with the Adversary (Satan)[1] standing at his right hand to accuse him." The author imagines a court scene in which the angel of the Lord represents God as judge and satan as prosecutor.

The familiar book of Job, apparently written in the fifth century B.C., illustrates this idea dramatically. Satan is among those present on certain court days when the

---

1. The word satan probably appears here for the first time. It is difficult to say how old is the tradition behind the text. The word satan has the same meaning in Psalm 108:6. The date of the Psalm is unknown.

heavenly beings assemble before God. His task is to roam the earth in the interests of Yahweh and to weigh the motives of men. Since he questions Job's inward sincerity and piety, God authorizes him to test Job's love. This authorization gives Satan control over such hostile forces as illnesses and natural disasters—powers far exceeding those customarily attributed to a prosecutor. Notice that in this story Satan is neither an evil spirit, a demon, nor a tempter to sin as he becomes in later thought. However, it is easy to see how such a character gradually developed into an evil being, for already in the book of Job Satan is man's antagonist and is cynical in his attitude toward both man and Yahweh.

In 1 Chronicles 21:1, written about 400 B.C.,[2] Satan "rose up against Israel and moved David to number Israel." David's taking a census of his people is displeasing to God, and we note that it is Satan who gave the suggestion to David. Thus we see that temptation to evil begins to be associated with the figure of Satan. This association developed out of the gradual refinement of the Hebrew notion of God. Originally the Hebrews ascribed evil acts as well as good to God, whom they saw as responsible for all that happened. Gradually they came to understand that evil could not come from God, and thus they developed the notion of an evil spirit with whom evil originated.[3]

---

2. 1 Chronicles 21:1 reinterprets 2 Samuel 24:1-3, a sixth century text.
3. As to the influence of the Persian religion on the biblical figure of Satan, G. von Rad says that the satan figure as such is not borrowed from the Persian religion. In fact, the Old Testament satan as prosecutor and adversary has no analogies even in Babylonian ideas. There is no parallel in the Persian religion to the legal powers

We also learn from 1 Chronicles that "satan" becomes a proper name for the devil rather than a name for the office. Previously the word was always written with the Hebrew article, "the satan," which means any adversary or accuser of another man. But in 1 Chronicles for the first time, the word appears without the article which means it appears as the proper name of this figure who is no longer known as the satan but as Satan.

A thorough perusal of the Old Testament should indicate that the notion of Satan is rare. He is neither of great importance nor a consistent figure in the Old Testament religion. For example, in all the texts presented so far, the people seem to think of satan as a vague spiritual being; in Numbers 22:22, on the other hand, a human being is spoken of as satan, namely, the pagan prophet Balaam.

The Serpent in Genesis

While the story of the creation and fall of man in Genesis was written as far back as the 10th century B.C., the identification of the serpent of the story with a devil or evil spirit did not take place until centuries later. In fact, except for an allusion in Wisdom 2:24 (c. 1st century B.C.),[4] the New Testament writers seem to have been the first to make this identification.[5] In the Genesis account

---

of the Old Testament satan. The Old Testament never teaches the ontological dualism of a good God and an evil god as does the Persian religion. On this question of foreign influence an exception must be made for the book of Tobit because it shows unquestionable influence of Persian demonological beliefs.
4. "But by the envy of the devil death entered the world."
5. Revelation 12:9 ". . . that ancient serpent, who is called the Devil and Satan." Cf. Romans 16:20; John 8:44.

of man's first sin, the author chose the serpent to represent the power of evil (*not* the devil) probably in order to show contempt for the serpent, which was an important element in the idolatrous fertility cults of contemporary pagan rites. The most significant passage for our purposes is Gn. 3:15: "I will put enmity between you [the serpent] and the woman [Eve] and between your offspring and hers. He will strike at your head, while you strike at his heel." This passage seems to mean that the power of evil, represented by the serpent, will continue to struggle with man throughout the centuries; but eventually man, the offspring of the woman, will emerge as the victor.

Demons and Evil Spirits

The biblical books written before the sixth century B.C. rarely mention demons. They played an insignificant role in the *official* religion of the Israelites. But in the superstitions of the people, the demons enjoyed more popularity. As in the societies of many of their contemporaries, there were various practices of magic, divination, and necromancy. For example, 1 Samuel 28 tells about Saul's asking the witch of Endor to call up from the dead the spirit of Samuel for consultation. It is not surprising, therefore, that only a few demons were known by name in Israel. Leviticus 16, dealing with the ritual of the day of expiation, has preserved the name of the desert demon, Azazel (probably originally a foreign demonic deity). Asmodeus is another demon known from the book of Tobit, written in the 4th or 3rd century B.C. He killed the seven husbands of Sara and was believed to have power over those with unruly sexual instincts. Almost all critics recognize Asmodeus as the demon Aesmadaeva who in the Persian religion is the demon of anger.

Whatever developments took place in demonology in Israel seem to have been influenced by contact with pagan cults such as that of Persia. The more the Israelites realized the creative and ruling power of God over visible and invisible creation, the more their religious leaders branded the cult of demons as idolatry (cf. Dt. 18:9-13). On the other hand, the more the sanctity and perfection of God was affirmed, the more there was a theoretical need for evil spirits as a cause for physical and moral evils. Such a cause would separate these evils from God's causality, leaving God as the sole cause for good. The development of this line of thought took place at the period just before and at the beginning of the Christian era.

The Stories of Lucifer and the Fallen Angels

"Lucifer" is commonly thought of as another name for "the devil" or Satan. However, there is no connection in the Bible between these two names. The identification of Lucifer with Satan and the stories of "the fallen angels" represent good examples of something that has occurred all too frequently in the development of Christian thought: An idea to which there is only the vaguest allusion in Scripture is taken up by some early formulator of Christian thought such as during the Patristic era. This thinker speculates about the idea in his writings and soon there develops an intricate system of "doctrines" about the idea in question, which system is "founded on Scripture and the authority of the Fathers." And so for centuries conscientious believers accept uncritically as "Gospel truth" an idea which actually originated in the mind of one thinker who, while he may have been intelligent, was nonetheless very limited by the intellectual milieu of his time.

Such a simple mistake as the identification of Lucifer and Satan has a rather complex history. In the eighth century B.C. the prophet Isaiah composed a dramatic taunt-song mocking a Babylonian king who was probably intended as a personification of Babylon (Is. 14:4-21). Verse 12 of the song reads: "How have you fallen from the heavens, O morning star, son of the dawn!" The source of the song may be a pagan myth of the "morning star" ascending over all other stars only to be dashed down by the splendor of the victorious sun. The Latin Vulgate translation of the Bible made by St. Jerome in the fourth or fifth century A.D. correctly translates the Hebrew word *helal* ("morning star") by the Latin word "lucifer" which literally means "light bearer" but is used in classical Latin to mean "morning star."

Later, the early Church writers Justin and Origen read the words of Jesus in Luke 10:18: ". . . I watched Satan fall from the sky like lightning" and accommodated the fallen "lucifer" of Isaiah's song to the "Satan" of Luke's text. Actually, the words of Luke do not even refer to Isaiah's passage. They refer to the report of the 72 disciples who have just informed Jesus of their success in expelling devils in his name. This report and other spiritual victories cause Jesus to declare that he has seen the beginning of the fall of Satan as a power in the world. Jesus' statement does not refer to a vision or to an alleged fall of Satan from heaven. Thus Origen's fabrication is entirely without justification in Scripture.[6]

The story of the "fall" of the angels is similarly lacking in scriptural foundation and also has a complex origin. In the obscure story told in Genesis 6:1-4 (written in the 10th century B.C.) there is a legend of "sons of God" (which the Hebrews understood as "angels") who had intercourse with mortal women. The offspring of these unions were giants. The writer of Genesis took over this pagan legend to develop his sketch of evil increasing in the world from Adam to Cain to Lamech and finally to these evil giants. There is no mention of angels in heaven who disobeyed God and were cast into hell.

The stories of sinful fallen angels are mostly a development which took place in the few centuries before and after the beginning of the Christian era. The Jewish apocryphal[7] book of Jubilees written in the second century B.C. contains the earliest version of these stories based on Genesis 6:14, though it is based on an earlier tradition. According to this version, a group of angels led by Azazel lusted after the daughters of men and sinned with them. They were imprisoned in an earthly abyss from which they are to be liberated on judgment day only to be thrown into an abyss of fire. Jubilees adds that the

---

6. The title "Lucifer" sung in the melodious Exultet of the Easter Vigil, does not come from Isaiah nor from Luke but from Revelation 22:16 ("I Jesus . . . am . . . the bright morning star Lucifer") and 2 Peter 1:19.

7. Apocryphal books are those books which were finally disqualified as inspired books belonging to the Bible.

demons are ranked under Satan as his fallen angels. Other apocryphal books give different versions of the Genesis legend.

The only New Testament references to the fall of angels are found in 2 Peter 2:4: ("God did not spare the angels who sinned but consigned them to the dark pits of hell where they are reserved for judgment") and in the epistle of Jude, 1:6: "There were angels, too, who did not keep to their own domain, who deserted their dwelling place. These the Lord has kept in perpetual bondage, shrouded in murky darkness against the judgment of the great day." Both are based on a story found in the apocryphal book of 1 Enoch, 10:4-6; 19:1; 54:3-5.

These apocryphal stories of Lucifer and the host of fallen angels lie behind the New Testament passages about the devil as head of all the demons. It is useful for us to investigate these stories because they help us to understand why the New Testament writers had the concepts they had—they were influenced by the stories of their times. However, based as they are on legend and apocryphal writings, these stories need not be considered part of the body of divine revelation which good Christians must cling to in faith.

Devils in the New Testament

The Greek words *satanas* for Satan and *diabolos* for devil are used interchangeably in the New Testament. The former occurs 36 times; the latter 34 times. Our English word "devil" comes from *diabolos*. The different New Testament writers each have their own favorite names. Matthew, Mark and Luke usually speak of Satan

or the devil and less frequently of the tempter, Beelzebub,[8] the prince of devils. John prefers the prince or ruler
of this world. St. Paul uses a variety of names, e.g., the
prince of the power of the air, the devil, Satan.

An outstanding characteristic of the New Testament
view of Satan or the devil is the antithesis between him
and God or Christ and between the kingdom of God in
Christ and the kingdom of Satan. The functions attributed to Satan in the Old Testament (accuser and hater
of man, tempter, opponent of God) are found again but
more emphatically in the New Testament writings where
they reach their apex in the concept of Satan as a single
power and ruler to whom demons are subject.

Jesus' entire ministry can be viewed as a prolonged bat-
tle with the forces of evil. At decisive moments in his life
Satan appears: in the desert just before he begins his mission of teaching; in the hostile atmosphere of the debates
with his Jewish opponents; at the end of his life when
Satan takes possession of Judas. In spite of Satan's aggres-
siveness, Jesus binds him and takes his goods. Thus Satan
loses his right to accuse men and Jesus assumes the role
of judge (Mt. 12:29).

Jesus' act of expelling devils by a simple command is
a sign that the Messiah has arrived: "But if it is by the
Spirit of God that I cast out demons, then the kingdom
of God has come upon you" (Mt. 12:28). Moreover, illnesses are often attributed to Satan or to demons. The
lady with a "spirit" of infirmity in Luke 13:11 is just one

---

8. Beelzebub, the name of the god of Accaron (2 Kings 1, 2). There
   is no satisfactory explanation of how it became the name of Satan.
   In Hebrew, it means "the lord of the flies."

example. Mental illnesses were more readily attributed to diabolical possession than were physical diseases. The inspired writers wrote according to the language and ideas of their day—otherwise they would not have been understood. Consequently, they depicted Jesus' exorcisms as a manner of liberating men from the fear of demons.

In the first days of the Christian community, the Christians saw Satan continuing his activity as described in the Gospels: "Peter said, 'Anania, why has Satan filled your heart to lie?" (Acts 5:3). The epistles of Paul as well as those of James, 1 Peter, and 1 John convey warnings against the wiles of Satan. Paul expresses the New Testament idea of Satan as the ruler of this world by calling him "the god of this world" (2 Cor. 4:4). Paul means that Satan claims in this world the honor that belongs to God. His goal is to destroy men by alienating them from God. During the last struggle God himself will give Satan the power to oppose him, but the community's trust in God will in no way be shipwrecked by this power.

A study of the New Testament points up how rare are references to devils and demons (except in cases of possession). H. A. Kelly draws the following conclusion about scriptural data on devils:[9]

> There is no systematic demonology present; that comes only later, and only at the cost of distorting the biblical data to Procrustean specifications. A common factor behind the biblical motifs is the need to describe intelligibly the cause of obstacles to human happiness. But the explanations are

---

9. *The Devil, Demonology, and Witchcraft,* p. 17.

invariably flavored by notions inherited or borrowed from cultures alien to Judaism.[10]

Recent Interpretations of the Biblical Data on Devils

Having surveyed the biblical roots of the Christian belief in devils, it is time for us to go back to the question asked in the beginning of this chapter: Is the existence of these beings a supposition based on the primitive world view held by the biblical writers? Is it intended to be part of the sacred revelation which they were inspired to write? Or did they merely assume the existence of devils without intending to *teach* this as a divinely revealed truth?

Some modern Catholic biblical scholars are beginning to call this idea into question and even to deny it, for reasons that should be apparent in the light of the above study, namely that the actual biblical texts which form the foundation of Christian teaching in this area are actually few and far between. These few texts simply show that the Hebrews popularly believed in these evil spirits,

---

10. Before concluding this section on devils in the New Testament a word must be said on Principalities and Powers. Ephesians 1:21 lists four cryptic names: Principality, Power, Virtue, Domination; and Colossians 1:16 adds thrones. The first four are abstract terms for angels, while the first three are used elsewhere for demons, e.g., Romans 8:38. The Ephesians and Colossians apparently believed in these astral powers or demonic world rulers as having an evil influence over human events and human destiny. Sometimes it seems that the Apostle did not believe in their existence. Paul tries to show that these beings do not wield the influence which the people attribute to them. The Apostle proclaims that Christ defeated them and thereby freed men from these malign powers.

but that their beliefs were for the most part not clearly formulated and rather resemble popular superstition than official religious teaching. The following conclusions of H. A. Kelly in *The Devil, Demonology and Witchcraft* represent this school of thought:

> We must conclude that a great deal of the demonology evolved under the name of Christian teaching can only be characterized as "untheological levity." The representations of the spirit world in Scripture betray signs of simple folkloristic origin, and the modification that these images and myths underwent when they came into contact with later cultures and philosophies are no longer convincing however satisfying they may have been for past ages. A continuing adherence to these views, as if they constituted an essential part of the divine revelation, runs the risk of exposing the whole Christian mission to ridicule. (p. 131)

Conclusions of Modern Systematic Theologians

In considering the Church's teaching as found in her writings from postbiblical times, it becomes obvious that the early Christians and those of the Middle Ages believed in the existence of devils. In fact, until modern times hardly anyone doubted that the Church taught this as a doctrine of faith. This remains the prevailing Catholic theological view of today.

However, some contemporary theologians do not believe that the existence of devils is part of revealed doctrine of faith but that it was always assumed or presupposed. According to Duquoc, the Church has never been "preoccupied in the defense of the existence of a personal Satan."[11] In a number of cases in which the doctrine of

---

11. *Lumière et Vie*, no. 78, 1966.

Satan's existence entered into a Church controversy, it has been not the existence of Satan which the Church affirmed, but rather some other teaching which merely assumed his existence. The decision of the Fourth Lateran Council in the year 1215 is most often cited in favor of the teaching on the existence of personal devils. The proposition in question reads: "For the devil and the other demons were created good by nature, by God, but of their own doing they became evil" (Denz. 428). However, one cannot thereby conclude that by implying the existence of devils the council thereby "implicitly defined their existence."[12] T. McDermott, O.P.[13] concludes:

> She (the Church) has not, as far as I can see, ever taught officially the reality of the devil in the way we normally take that phrase. She has often taught the reality of "the power of the devil"; the Church has taught that the devils were created by God good in nature. Does this imply a real personal being called the devil? It must be remembered that what the Church is doing is *correcting* a tradition: the Manichean tradition that the principle of evil is uncreated and equal with God.

To summarize the opinions stated above, we may say that it appears that the Scriptures, ecclesiastical documents and tradition have only adopted the popular assumptions about the existence of devils, but have not intended that their existence be part of God's revealed message nor part of the object of our faith and belief. It seems that the revealed doctrine contained in the relevant texts is the underlying theology of God's power to

12. *Cf. Theological Dictionary,* Rahner & Vorgrimler, p. 127; *Sacramentum Mundi,* vol. I, p. 32.
13. *New Blackfriars,* 1966, p. 25.

conquer evil in the Old Testament, and Jesus conquering evil in the New Testament. In answering our original question, "Does the devil exist?" we may state that the evidence of Scripture merely shows that the Israelites of the Old Testament popularly held to a belief in evil spirits, but this belief was never part of their official body of revealed truths. Jesus and the writers of the New Testament assumed these popular notions into their teachings about evil and God's power to conquer it without ever explicitly teaching the existence of the devil. The early and medieval Church took these presuppositions about the existence of the devil uncritically and added to the scanty scriptural notions a rather involved body of speculation which later generations of Christians assumed to be truth revealed in Scripture. Therefore, it seems unnecessary for committed Christians to hold to the belief in devils as an object of faith. It must be made clear that a denial of the devils as personal spiritual beings is not thereby a denial of real evil in the world that affects us personally, both individually and collectively.

It is worth noting that just as it is legitimate to reinterpret Scripture in the light of natural sciences, e.g., as in the question of creation in six days, so is it legitimate to reinterpret Scripture in the light of the sociological and psychological sciences as in the problem of devil(s).

Related Problems

What must we conclude about related problems of devil(s) in witchcraft, in cases of possession, in temptations, and in the liturgy?

In his book, *Towards the Death of Satan,* H. A. Kelly concludes:

> We have no good reason to suppose that demons exist unless we have evidence of their actions. In former times they were believed to be active in witchcraft, diabolical possession, and diabolical temptation. But nowadays, witchcraft is nonexistent, "diabolical possession" is explained psychologically and temptation can never be proved to be diabolical. In earlier centuries the diagnosis was probably incorrect. Therefore belief in demons is without sufficient foundation.

Although witchcraft is still alive, Kelly most likely means that it is nonexistent as a scientifically tenable practice.

In light of our present understanding there may be a further toning down of the mention of devil(s) in the liturgical exorcisms found in the baptismal services and in the formulas for blessing holy water and other sacramentals. Pending this liturgical reform, the references to the devil(s) may be reinterpreted as references to evil.

IV

Is Hell Eternal?

The existence of an eternal hell is an idea offensive to many Christians today. A God who understands and compassionates man seems far more worthy of man's love and devotion than a God who judges and condemns. The god who casts fire and brimstone on his trembling creatures is a dead god of Greek mythology, not the God that Jesus spoke of *as his father*. And many would question whether man is really capable of the kind of choices which would reject God forever. New developments in the field of psychology make moral theologians reconsider the limits of the freedom which man brings to each of his moral choices.

Where Did Our Notion of Hell Come From?

In the Bible there are four terms that are related to our idea of hell:[1] *sheol, hades, gehenna,* and *tartarus.*

---

1. The English word "hell" comes from the German "hel" which means the realm of the dead deprived of God's company.

Sheol is an early Old Testament word. The ancient Near Eastern writers pictured a three-story universe consisting of the heavens, the earth and the subterranean world. The subterranean world was pictured as an ocean under the earth. Toward the bottom of the ocean was sheol. Synonyms for the Hebrew word sheol in the Old Testament are "the pit" and "the grave."

Sheol is the place of no return for wicked and just alike. It is miserably full of darkness, dust and worms. There is no activity in sheol, for nobody works there. It is a place of oblivion. No one remembers or praises God. This is the meaning of Psalm 6:6: "For among the dead no one remembers you; in the nether world who gives you thanks?" The gloomy inhabitants of this world do not remember Yahweh nor does he remember them. Yahweh's fidelity and wondrous deeds are not remembered there. To intensify the atmosphere of gloom, sheol is sometimes described in terms of a Mesopotamian palace-fortress with chambers, gates and bars.

The notion of sheol does not describe a kind of "life after death" but is rather used as "a picturesque denial of all that is meant by life and activity."[2] In other words, rather than depicting a continuation of existence, sheol simply represents death. The phrase "to go down to sheol" means to die, and the phrase "to bring down to sheol" means to kill. "Sheol then for the Hebrew is not a place of torment for the wicked after death, but the state of death itself which overcomes both just and wicked alike. . . . Sheol then is nothing more nor less than the

---

2. J. L. McKenzie S.J., *Dictionary of the Bible*, p. 800.

state of being dead, presented metaphorically as a place, but described in images that refer above all to the state. . . . Sheol is death as utter negation of life, as the sheer dead-end. The images are images of nothingness, saying nothing positive about it at all. If sheol is conceived as a place, it is because it is the ultimate no-place."[3]

In the latter years of the Old Testament, there developed the notion of God rewarding the good and punishing the wicked. This development led to the idea of sheol having separate divisions for the good and the wicked. A passage which hints at this idea is a dirge over Egypt made by the prophet Ezekiel April 27, 585 B.C (Ez. 32:17-32). This epic-like dirge describes the mighty warriors of history scornfully greeting Egypt, a newcomer to sheol: ". . . then from the midst of the nether world, the mighty warriors shall speak to Egypt: 'Whom do you excel in beauty? Come down, you and your allies, lie with the uncircumcised, with those slain by the sword.' . . . They do not lie with the mighty men fallen of old, who went down to the nether world with their weapons of war, whose swords were placed under their heads and whose shields were laid over their bones, though the mighty men caused terror in the land of the living. But in the midst of the uncircumcised shall you lie, with those slain by the sword" (Ez. 32:18-19, 27-28).

In the Septuagint Greek translation of the Old Testament, sheol is twice translated by "death" and every other

3. T. McDermott, O.P., *New Blackfriars*, "Hell," vol. 48, p. 188, January, 1967.

time by "hades." Death, hades and sheol are terms always
linked together. It follows then, that whenever we read
the word "hades" in the New Testament, we should think
of sheol, the *state* of death rather than a definite *place* of
punishment after death. One New Testament example of
this usage is the words of Christ to Peter: "And I also say
to you, you are Peter and upon this rock I will build my
church and the gates of *hell* will not prevail against it"
(Mt. 16:18). Since the Greek word translated "hell" is
"hades," the more modern translations say something like
this: "and the powers of *death* shall not prevail against it"
(RSV). The meaning is that the Church will not fall into
the power of sheol, which means that she will not die.
Another usage of the terms is in Acts 2:31, when Peter
says that Christ was not abandoned "in hades." Peter
means that Jesus did not remain in the power of sheol, of
death, because "this Jesus God raised up" (2:32).

Another biblical word related in meaning to hell is
"gehenna" which comes from the Aramaic and Hebrew
Ge Hinnom, the valley of Hinnom. This valley was located at the southern end of Jerusalem. During the eighth
and seventh centuries B.C., at a place in this valley called
Thopheth, children were burned in sacrifice to the pagan
god Moloch. The prophet Jeremiah says: "In the valley
of Ben-Hinnom they have built the high place of Thopheth to immolate in fire their sons and daughters, such a
thing as I never commanded" (Jer. 7:31). Later this valley became the "town dump." In extrabiblical literature
from the second century B.C. onward, this valley became
synonymous with the hell of the last judgment. Threats
of judgment proclaimed by the prophets concerned this

dismal valley as a place of punishment, and eventually as the fiery hell at the end-time. By the time of Christ, the word "gehenna" had evolved from a topographical term to a religious term, i.e., the place of punishment for the wicked after death. Gehenna is a place of "unquench-able fire" (Mk 9:43) "where their worm does not die and the fire is not quenched" (Mk 9:48). Probably the worm is a metaphor for the reproach of personal conscience.

Tartarus, the fourth term related to the idea of hell, is not found in the Old Testament at all and only once in the New Testament. Used by Greek writers around the begin-ning of the Christian era, tartarus was a mythological sub-terranean abode lower than hades where the Titans and the enemies of the gods were punished. The author of the second epistle of Peter uses the term to signify the place to which the fallen angels were banished: "For if God did not spare the angels when they sinned, but cast them down to Tartarus, and committed them to the dark pits to await judgment" (2 Pt. 2:4). Other than what is stated above, it is difficult to show a relation between tartarus on the one hand and sheol–hades–gehenna on the other.

How to Interpret the "Last Things"?

In the interpretation of scriptural texts on hell and the other "last things," purgatory, heaven, judgment, there are three possible approaches. One is the fundamentalist approach which accepts all the words at face value and uncritically. In this interpretation, "fire of hell" would be understood as the same kind of fire which can burn physi-cal realities. The other extreme approach would reject not only the images but all the reality so that hell does not exist even as a state. Karl Rahner speaks thus against this radical approach:

> The Christian understanding of the faith and its expression must contain an eschatology which really bears on the future, that which is still to come, in a very ordinary, empirical sense of the word time. An interpretation of the eschatological assertions of Scripture, which in the course of simply de-mythizing it would de-eschatologize it in such a way that all eschatological sayings of Scripture, explicit or implicit, only meant something that takes place here and now in the existence of the individual and in the decision he takes here and now, is theologically unacceptable.[4]

What we may call the third approach by Rahner is by far the best because it is more faithful to the meaning of the New Testament.

Truth versus Imagery

In considering the scriptural terms related to our concept of hell, we are faced with the difficult task of separating truth from imagery. Biblical interpreters generally agree that these terms *are* images, and that one ought not conclude that for example, gehenna, is actually a place burning with real fire. Likewise, the "unquenchableness" of the fire refers to the quality of the punishment, rather than its duration—the quality of finality, irrevocableness.

What Does the Church Officially Teach about Hell?

The official Church teaching on the doctrine of hell can be summarized in this way: hell exists, its punishment be-

---

4. K. Rahner, *Theological Investigations,* Vol. VI, p. 326.

gins immediately after death, and it lasts forever.[5] Nothing is said about the nature of the punishment, such as its consisting of a physical fire. The teaching that it begins immediately after death without awaiting the Last Judgment is consistent with the notion of hades discussed above. The teaching that hell is eternal is an affirmation that "human life is threatened by the real possibility of eternal shipwreck, because man freely disposes of himself and can therefore freely refuse himself to God."[6] Whether or not man actually does reject God with finality is a question about which the Church has made no pronouncement, and indeed can have no knowledge. The Church teaches about hell not to satisfy man's curiosity about his destiny but to lead him to conversion. While eternal perdition remains a possibility for man, it is also possible that relatively few men actually do evil to the extent of being deserving of eternal punishment.

What Are Modern Catholic Thinkers Questioning?

The biggest problem for the thinking Catholic is how an all-merciful God can condemn anyone to punishment that lasts forever. The answer to this problem lies in focusing not on God's apparent lack of mercy, but on man's free will to accept or reject God's mercy. This freedom makes it possible for man to reject God with finality and never to be reconciled. There will be no conversion after death: "Man can choose to make death an ultimate cul-

5. Denzinger, *Enchiridion Symbolorum,* ed. K. Rahner, 1960; numbers 16, 40, 429, 464, 714, 531, 211.
6. K. Rahner, H. Vorgrimler, eds. *Theological Dictionary,* p. 201f.

de-sac, if he wishes; this is what the doctrine of the eternity of hell is teaching. The Church says to us: do not deceive yourselves into thinking that all cul-de-sacs have their hidden openings, that you are not capable of rejecting God. Hell is precisely defined as the road of no return."[7]

Conclusions

Hell is not a place but a state; punishment begins immediately after death; the fire and flames of hell are not to be understood literally nor are "exterior darkness," "worm," "weeping and gnashing of teeth," "burning pit," "furnace of fire," and "lake of fire." The nature of the punishment of hell, symbolized by fire, does not consist in a vengeful God tormenting sinners. Instead of understanding hell's punishment as "separation from God," we should emphasize man's part in alienating himself from God. In the novel *The Great Divorce* by C. S. Lewis, one who has just died is wandering about in hell, speaking with the damned. The newcomer is informed that there is no torture in hell—rather that each man is his own oppressor because of the knowledge he possesses, his consciousness of guilt. Hell is the abode of wrath where no one suffers on another's account, but instead tortures himself with the memory of malice ever present in his own mind.

The most difficult problem about the question of hell remains, namely, the notion of its eternity. Is man really capable of evil to the extent of deserving a penalty which

---

7. T. McDermott, *art. cit.,* p. 196.

is in a sense infinite? And could not God, without infringing upon personal liberty, prevent a person from falling into hell? Theologians such as Karl Rahner insist that eternal hell is possible. Whether or not there are actually any human beings who merit an eternal hell is a question to which they imply a negative answer.

A final question to consider is the meaning of the liturgical sayings on hell. Scripture is constantly being reinterpreted in the light of new findings, and the scriptural texts quoted explicitly or implicitly in the liturgy must likewise be reinterpreted. One example of a text referring to hell is in the number one canon of the Mass, just before the consecration: "Save us from *eternal* damnation." This petition may be interpreted as a plea to be saved from freely rejecting God forever. There are several references to hell in the liturgy for funerals and the dead, and they may be similarly interpreted.

V

Polygenesis and
Original Sin

Of all the doctrinal problems with which modern theologians and Christians have had to contend, probably none is more controversial than the interpretation of the doctrine of original sin. As most Christians are aware, the problem centers around the interpretation of the first three chapters of Genesis, which tell the story of "the creation and fall of man," and the reconciling of this scriptural text with the modern scientific theories of evolution. As long as one holds to an evolutionary theory which is based on some form of monogenesis (i.e. the evolution of the entire human race from *one* original human pair) it is not too difficult to reconcile the Genesis story and the traditional belief in original sin with such a theory. But today, most scientists hold (and though they cannot conclusively prove it, the evidence strongly supports them) that the evolution of the human race happened polygenetically, i.e. that of the several or many members of the human species evolved more or less simultaneously and independently of each other.

When this theory first began to receive widespread acceptance, the reaction of Catholics was simply to deny the possibility of polygenesis. In 1950, Pope Pius XII wrote an encyclical entitled *On the Origins of Mankind* (*Humani Generis*) which warned against the implications of the theory of polygenesis, which he conceived of as contradictory to the doctrine of original sin. But today, theologians are realizing that it will do no good to continue to cling blindly to a theory of monogenesis when science is finding more and more evidence of the polygenetic origins of the human race. The problem today, then, is to reconsider the doctrine of the creation and fall of man in relation to the possibility of polygenesis.

In this chapter, we will summarize the traditional presentation of the doctrine of original sin as developed in relation to monogenetic evolutionary theory, present a few of the more plausible theories of modern theologians accepting polygenesis as a possibility, and reconsider the essence of the doctrine of original sin in this light.

Traditional Teaching on Original Sin

The Church's traditional presentation of the doctrine of original sin is based primarily on two biblical passages: the first three chapters of Genesis, and a passage from Paul's epistle to the Romans. Presuming the reader to be familiar with the Genesis creation story, we will quote here only the relevant passage from Romans 5:12-19:

> Therefore, just as through one man sin entered the world and with sin death, death thus coming to all men inasmuch as all sinned—before the law there was sin in the world even though sin is not imputed when there is no law—I say, from Adam to Moses death reigned, even over those who

had not sinned by breaking a precept as did Adam, that type of the man to come. But the gift is not like the offense. For if by the offense of the one man all died, much more did the grace of God and the gracious gift of the one man, Jesus Christ, abound for all. The gift is entirely different from the sin committed by the one man. In the first case, sentence followed upon one offense and brought condemnation, but in the second, the gift came after many offenses and brought acquittal. If death began its reign through one man because of his offense, much more shall those who receive the overflowing grace and gift of justice live and reign through the one man, Jesus Christ.

To sum up, then: just as a single offense brought condemnation to all men, a single righteous act brought all men acquittal and life. Just as through one man's disobedience all became sinners, so through one man's obedience all shall become just.

Based upon the most obvious (and uncritical) interpretation of these two passages, the doctrine of original sin was presented thus: Adam was a single person from whom all human beings have descended through actual physical generation. Adam (and Eve) lived in a state of happiness in which they were endowed with the "preternatural" gifts (i.e. gifts exceeding what is natural to man) of wholeness—by which their appetites were under perfect control of reason—and immortality. Adam and Eve sinned at a specific place and time causing a condition of sin in every man before he sins personally; or—to state it another way—effectively cutting the entire human race off from the grace they would have received had Adam not sinned. It is obvious that this theory depends upon a monogenetic evolution of the human race.

Had the first man accepted God's original gift of supernatural life, all men would have been born in the state of grace and into a world wherein people lived according to supernatural love. Men would have developed in an environment where human nature was subject to reason and reason was subject to God. Finally, they would have passed from life on earth to life in the next world without the catastrophic experience of death as we know it.

But because the first man sinned, evolution took a different direction. God still intended for man to partake of the glory of eternal life through the fruits of the life and death of Jesus. Through his union with Christ, man would still be able to gain control over his human nature. But full control and holiness would be perfect only in the afterlife when even death would be surmounted. Meanwhile, even after man receives grace, he still falls into sin.

New Approaches to Original Sin

For the past decade, theologians have been giving consideration to the possibility of polygenesis. Biblical scholars have been showing with increasing clarity that Genesis 1-3 and Romans 5:12-19, if correctly interpreted, are compatible with polygenesis. They have also reexamined the Church's teaching on original sin to find that polygenesis is not incompatible with the essential core of the doctrine of original sin. We will present below the explanations given by three prominent theologians.

Karl Rahner's Thesis

Karl Rahner[1] approaches the problem from a negative point of view, that is, by trying to show that the theory of

---

1. "Evolution and Original Sin," in *The Evolving World and Theology*, ed. by J. Metz, vol. 26 of Concilium, pp. 61-73.

polygenism and the doctrine of original sin are not mutually exclusive. He shows that the Old Testament provides neither a direct nor an indirect proof of monogenism: "If we interpret Genesis 1-3 correctly according to its literary genre and consider how man's (and therefore, the *first* man's) origin is revealed—that is, as a retrospective view of how man came about—the Old Testament tells us nothing about monogenism."[2] The New Testament basically only repeats the Old Testament in this regard. Even Paul to the Romans is merely assuming—not explicating —the Old Testament ideas on the origin of man. Likewise, Rahner states that monogenism has never as such been defined by the Church as a dogma: "It is true that the Council of Trent presupposed an 'Adam who is physically one.' " But in this case it was speaking of original sin and simply repeating the statement of Scripture and tradition. It did not define monogenism since this question was neither put nor intended" (p. 63). Even the encyclical *Humani Generis* (cited above) does not assume that monogenism is a dogma of the magisterium and therefore irrevocable.

Having concluded that monogenism cannot be proved from the Old and New Testaments, and that it has never been defined as a dogma by the magisterium, Rahner proposes the following thesis: "In the present state of theology and science it cannot be proved that polygenism conflicts with orthodox teaching on original sin. It would therefore be better if the magisterium refrained from censuring polygenism" (p. 64). He begins his exposition by showing that, if the Church allows us to accept evolutionary hominization in the case of Adam, then we must

---

2. P. 62.

also conclude that "Eve" came about in the same way as
"Adam." Thus we already have polygenism in the case of
this one couple. It then seems very unlikely that—of all
the members of the prehuman species—only two should
break through to become the first human beings. However, if several or many members of the species evolved
simultaneously, they would nonetheless have formed a
biological and historical unit "achieved through a genu-
inely possible personal communication process" (p. 68).
This being the case, Rahner presents arguments showing
that it is conceivable either that *one* man within this
group, or the group collectively, through sin blocked "the
grace-transmitting function which accompanied human
descent from this group" (p. 69).

Thus Rahner concludes that it is not necessary to maintain a monogenetic theory of human origins; and that a
polygenetic view in which the original group was a biological and historical unit can be reconciled with the
traditional belief in original sin.

Piet Schoonenberg

In his book *Man and Sin,*[3] Piet Schoonenberg takes a
relatively conservative approach to the question of polygenism but considers the matter unsettled. According to
Schoonenberg,

> Both the magisterium and those who listen to it must realize
> that what matters is not to cling to a formula, but to be
> faithful to a message. We do not need a formula which may

---

3. Schoonenberg, P., *Man and Sin,* University of Notre Dame Press,
Notre Dame, Ind., 1965.

be repeated mechanically, but a message of salvation, with everything it includes (in the present case a message of doom), which must be announced amidst the changing circumstances of human history (p. 168).

Schoonenberg asserts that the Council of Trent, which defined the doctrine of original sin, does not make monogenism a doctrine of faith, nor do the ecclesiastical doctrinal statements of the last century when the question really came to the fore. He considers that the presumption is in favor of the doctrine of monogenism, but that polygenism may still be reconcilable with the doctrine of original sin.

Schoonenberg's particular contribution is his theology of "the sin of the world." This "sin of the world" is not identical with original sin, but Schoonenberg suggests that perhaps what is needed in modern theology is an elaboration or broadening of the teaching on original sin, which the concept of the "sin of the world" would provide. The notion of the sin of the world is based upon the fact of human solidarity, a concept central to the entire biblical notion of sin. It refers to the "situatedness" of man in a world of sin. This sin is more than the sum total of all the individual sins of men. It is the condition in which man is affected from all sides by the sins of other men, with the result that men are "affected in their own liberty" (p. 105). This situation includes the elements of bad example, bad example with pressure, obscuring of values and norms—in other words, a total environment pervaded by sin. This sin of the world reached its fullness in the world's rejection and killing of Christ and the resulting creation of "the abyss of death" between us and him (p. 123).

Schoonenberg believes that this notion of the sin of the world implies a number of elements which could fruitfully be integrated with the classic doctrine of original sin:

> Scripture speaks of the sinfulness of all men not only in connection with "Adam," for the very texts which speak of "Adam" mention a more sinful influence than that which derives from one first ancestor alone. To this we must add that our whole conception of the world urgently inquires whether the extraordinary importance which the classic doctrine attributes to the chronologically first man is really deserved, nay, whether we may speak of one first ancestor of the human race at all. The classic doctrine does not seem to take sufficiently into account not only the humble condition of him or of those who crossed the threshold into the human estate but also God's universal salvific will for mankind between "Adam" and Abraham, and the historical circumstances in which it takes shape (p. 177).

The author suggests that the notion of the sin of the world removes the sin of Adam from "isolation," and deemphasizes the *beginning* of life—whether of the individual or of the race—as the focal point of sin; and it makes the influence of Adam's sin upon all succeeding generations of men much more comprehensible than the notion of the simple passing on by physical generation of a grace-less condition within the individual.

Schoonenberg leaves open the question as to whether original sin and the sin of the world may be equated, and he sees a number of difficulties involved in making this identification.[4] Leaving aside that question, we will simply point out that a consideration of the notion of the sin

---

4. Cf. pp. 181-191.

of the world—whether or not it can be equated with original sin—makes the belief in a single original human ancestor much less important, and thus makes polygenesis more plausible even with the traditional doctrine of original sin.

A. M. Dubarle

In *The Biblical Doctrine of Original Sin,* A. M. Dubarle[5] also leaves the possibility of polygenism an open question. Dubarle suggests the possibility of an interpretation of the origin of sin which lies between two extremes: on the one hand, the usual interpretation of Gn. 3 as an account of a specific sin "at the beginning which had consequences for the whole of mankind" (p. 226); and on the other hand the proposal by some modern exegetes "who see in Chapter 3 of Genesis only the stylized outline of individual sin" (p. 226). Dubarle explains his "middle" position as follows:

> In Genesis the characteristics and the destiny of different peoples or tribes are traced back to the action of one ancestor giving to each his name and his psychological characteristics. . . . The biblical authors were very conscious of the connection between the successive links of a line. In their eyes the divine choice was conditioned by membership of a particular race. And conversely the faults of an individual were visited on his children and their children to the third and fourth generation. (Ex. 20:5; 34:7; Dt. 5:9; Nm. 14-18; Jer. 32:18). So they were able to portray in one single ancestor and the sentence pronounced on his descend-

5. Dubarle, A. M., *The Biblical Doctrine of Original Sin.* Herder & Herder, N.Y., 1964.

ants the common effect of multiple sins, the consequence of disturbances which go on diminishing. It is then possible that the whole of mankind with the constant factors of its condition, was consciously represented in the story of Adam, whose name means "man" (pp. 223-224).

Dubarle goes on to point out (and we note his similarity to Schoonenberg) that such an explanation of the Genesis account draws the emphasis away from the notion of "a unique catastrophe at the birth of our species" (p. 224) and makes the influence of the sin of Adam upon future generations much more plausible. In regard to the question of polygenesis, Dubarle leaves it open, but implies that the intention of the author of Genesis, the intention of Paul and of the Council of Trent was to emphasize not "the strict unity of origin of the human race" but rather "the universality of sin" (p. 228).

The Essence of the Doctrine of Original Sin

From the above presentation of the theories of three theologians, we may conclude that polygenism does not contradict the doctrine of original sin and that the two ideas may be considered compatible. What, then, ought we to consider to be the essential core of the doctrine of original sin? There are several elements: at the beginning of the human race, evil and sin were introduced into the world by the free decision of man. The effect of this "original" sin reaches to every man born into the human race, even before he has a chance to ratify it by his personal sins. This situation of sin affecting every man puts every man in need of redemption by Christ.

Thus far in our presentation there has been no discussion of the condition of man before his sin. The traditional explanation supposed that before his sin, the first man lived in a state of grace and happiness, possessing a sort of "preternatural perfection," including physical immortality. Most modern thinkers find it impossible to harmonize such a theory with the evolutionary development of the human species. Such an idealized picture of the original state of primordial man is nowhere defined by the Church, nor intended by the biblical passages. We may end with Dubarle's summary statement: ". . . Without contradicting any irrevocable doctrinal authority, scriptural or ecclesiastical, we can, in conformity with the suggestions of the evolution theory, admit that mankind emerged from the animal world."[6]

---

6. Op. cit, p. 236. The three theories of Rahner, Schoonenberg and Dubarle illustrate the possibility of polygenism in relation to original sin. The theory of Alszeghy-Flick concerns itself with *how* polygenism might have happened—a question whose answer belongs to the scientist, not the theologian. For the child-men theory of Alszeghy-Flick see the author's article, "Polygenesis and Original Sin", *The Homiletic and Pastoral Review,* Vol. 68, No. 1, Oct. 1967, pp. 17-22.

VI

Did Jesus Christ
Found a Church?

If Jesus were to return to the world today and ask the members of the Catholic Church "Is this the church I founded?" would he receive the same answer which the Grand Inquisitor gave in Dostoevski's *Brothers Karamazov* to the returning Christ: "Why do you come to disturb us?" Many Christian scholars are no longer satisfied with what "tradition" says about Jesus founding a church with Peter as its first bishop (of Rome) and a strict line of apostolic succession of popes and bishops. These scholars are investigating the *origins* of this tradition. Charles Davis, for example, asserts that Jesus never founded any church, let alone the Catholic Church. And Hans Küng, in his controversial book *The Church,* does not defend the Catholic Church as the "one true Church."

The Origin of the Christian Church

What is meant by "church"? For Catholics, a standard meaning of "church" is the body of those who are in allegiance to the pope of Rome. But this is a late definition of church. We must consider the meaning of "church" as it was understood at the time of Jesus. To say that Jesus founded a church during his lifetime would mean that he formed a specific group with a specific rule required for membership. Did Jesus found such a group?

Many Christian scholars answer that Jesus did not found a church during his lifetime or during the pre-Easter period.[1] There are a number of convincing reasons for this opinion, but there are also a number of objections to it which must be answered. An argument *for* this opinion is that an announcement by Jesus of an intention to found a church would have been interpreted by his Jewish audience as an intention to found a separate synagogue. This would have weakened and confused his message in their minds. And besides, Jesus preached to *all* the people and not merely to a select group. Nor did he ever set down anything like "membership rules" for a select society.

It may be objected at this point that Jesus selected the specific group of the twelve apostles as the nucleus of his "church." Some scholars claim that the evangelists *attributed* the choosing of these twelve to Jesus but that he did not really choose these men as a separate and distinct group. However, let us concede that he did. Even so, Jesus founded the group of the twelve as representative of all Israel. The Jewish Christians of Jesus' day looked upon his selection of twelve apostles as a clarion call to

---

1. For the sake of brevity, we shall not consider the opinion of those who deny that Jesus *ever* established a church, before or after Easter (e.g. R. Bultmann). Likewise, we shall discount the opinion of those (e.g. K. Stendahl) who consider the fact unknowable and unimportant.

all the descendants of the twelve tribes with the twelve apostles as their rulers or judges at the end of time. For example, Mt. 19:28 reads: "I give you my solemn word, in the new age when the Son of Man takes his seat upon a throne befitting his glory, you who have followed me shall likewise take your places on twelve thrones to judge the twelve tribes of Israel."

The objection that Jesus called the wider group of "disciples" as the select members of his church may be answered in similar fashion: they were entrusted with the mission to preach to *all* the people. Neither the apostles nor the disciples were given a specific rule of life to qualify them as strict members of a church.

The words of Jesus in Matthew 16:18 provide the basis for another objection: "I for my part declare to you, you are 'Rock' and on this rock I will build my church, and the jaws of death shall not prevail against it." Disregarding the question of whether or not Jesus himself said this, and the difficulties of interpretation, one fact is clear from the context of Matthew: this is not a statement made in public but it was made in private to the apostles only. Because of this fact, the use of this verse is not a very cogent argument in favor of the position that Jesus founded a (public) church.

Another text which may be used as an objection is Matthew 18:17: "If he ignores them, refer it to the church. If he ignores even the church, then treat him as you would a Gentile or a tax collector." However, in this text the word "church" (ecclesia) refers merely to the local assembly of believers and not to a public church.

In traditional theology, the idea of the church has been deduced from the description of the reign of God in the

so-called "parables of the kingdom" (e.g. the parables of
the leaven (Mt. 13:33) and the fishnet (Mt. 13:47-50).
But this reign of God is described as futuristic, not as a
temporal reign of God on earth intended to develop into
a church.

In considering the above objections and discounting
them, we are left with little evidence that Jesus founded
a church before Easter. We may however, concede that
he did lay the foundation for his church in this period,
though that church did not take shape until after Easter.
He laid this foundation by preaching and ministering to
all the people rather than organizing followers into a
definite sect such as were the sects of the Pharisees and
Sadducees.

If we are concluding that Jesus' church was not formed
until after Easter, then when specifically did it appear?
The church of Jesus began when the apostles and their
followers believed—through faith—in Jesus' resurrection, when they believed that he rose and would come
again in glory at the end of the world. It was not from a
particular word or speech of Jesus after the resurrection
that the Church originated; but rather his person, preaching, and ministry were themselves the origin of the
Church.

Peter as Head of the Church

Having concluded that Jesus' church began after Easter (without having adequately dealt with all the problems involved in this conclusion) we come now to the
problem of whether Jesus made Peter the head of this
post-Easter church.

The Scripture text traditionally used to answer this question is Matthew 16:18: "I for my part declare to you, you are 'Rock' and on this rock I will build my church, and the jaws of death shall not prevail against it." The long-standing interpretation by the Roman Catholic Church has been that Jesus founded the church on the *person* of Peter. However, an interpretation which used to be opposed by Catholics and is now more sympathetically received explains the text in this way: Peter *is* the rock upon which the church is to be built, but not in the sense that the church is built on his *person*. The context of verse 18 gives the key: In his reply to Jesus' question, "Who do men say that the Son of Man is?" Peter asserts that Jesus is "the Christ (i.e. the Messiah), the son of the living God." In other words, the context shows Peter answering in the name of the group of apostles, and it is on Peter as the rock of *faith* that Jesus will build his church. The church will be built on the faith of Peter, not on his person. Consequently, as long as this faith of Peter in Jesus endures, the church will not die. Hence Jesus praises and recognizes the faith of Peter as divinely inspired: "Simon, son of Jonah, you are favored indeed! You did not learn that from mortal man; it was revealed to you by my heavenly Father." Consequently, if the church is not founded on the person of Peter, and it is not, then the Roman Catholic position of the successions of popes falls.

Even if Jesus had established his church on the person of Peter, would it follow that according to Jesus every successor of Peter was to be head of the Church?

O. Cullmann, a famous Protestant Scripture scholar, rightly claims that the biblical text of Matthew proves only that *Peter* is the head, but does not prove anything about his successors. Catholics generally answer that Peter was elected by Jesus and also *represents* all his successors. This "representation" idea seems to be forcing the biblical text.

The problem of Peter's successors raises four historical questions related to Peter's being the first bishop of Rome. In the past, Catholic scholars have tended to disregard these questions, but they are now taking a hard look at them: Was Peter ever even in Rome, and what is the historical evidence? *Did* Peter found the church in Rome? Was Peter the first bishop of Rome or even a "bishop" at all? Was Peter martyred in Rome? Recent historical investigations have shed important light in this area, an area which is significant because of its relation to the traditional Catholic concepts of the Church and the papacy.

The evidence of Peter's residing in Rome typically given is the text of the first epistle of Peter 5:13: "The church that is in Babylon, chosen together with you, sends you greeting. . . ." It has long been said that "Babylon" signifies Rome in the apocalyptic writings of the Jews.[2] Therefore, "The church which is at Babylon" has been interpreted to refer to the Church at *Rome* from which Peter is allegedly writing. There are several difficulties with this interpretation. The epistle of 1 Peter is not written in apocalyptic style. Many scholars do not even think that Peter wrote this epistle. Furthermore, it is only a conjecture to interpret "another place" in Acts

---

2. "Apocalyptic" refers to a literary form of writing which deals with the coming of the kingdom of God in a future and final period of world history.

12:17b as a reference to Rome: "Then he (Peter) departed and went to another place." In his book *Peter in Rome,* D. W. O'Connor investigates all the literary and archeological evidence and concludes that it cannot be proven that Peter was ever in Rome; of course, likewise it cannot be proven that Peter was never in Rome.[3]

Hardly any historians believe that Peter founded the church in Rome. In all probability, the "visitors from Rome" mentioned in Acts 2:10, who attended the Pentecost celebration in Jerusalem returned as the founders of the Christian group in Rome.

The assertion that Peter was bishop of Rome for twenty-five years is a legend no longer found in historical works but only in pious literature. This legend does not go back earlier than the third century. Monarchical episcopacy does not even exist in New Testament times, but originated in the second century. Not even claims stemming from Antioch claimed Peter as the bishop of that city. This is somewhat surprising since we know from Galatians 2:11 that Peter went to Antioch: "But when Cephas (Peter) came to Antioch . . ."

Was Peter martyred in Rome? Gaius (165 A.D.), a Roman Christian, is often quoted in history books as saying in a fragment in Eusebius' *Ecclesiastical History,* II 25.7: "I can show you the trophies (tombs) of the apostles (Peter and Paul)". It is likely that Gaius refers to the Aedicula (shrine) on the Vatican hill. But this testimony means only that Gaius believed that Peter (and

---

3. *The literary, liturgical and archaeological evidence* by D. W. O'Connor, pp. xiv and 242; 44 plates; New York: Columbia University Press, 1969.

Paul) were buried there; it does not prove this as a fact. D. W. O'Connor draws the following conclusion:

> If it is found that there is insufficient evidence that Peter was buried beneath the Aedicula on the Vatican, it is not proved thereby that he is not buried somewhere else on the Vatican Hill. If, in addition, it could be proved which it cannot, that Peter was never buried on the Vatican Hill or at San Sebastiano (catacomb), that his body had not been thrown into the Tiber and further that he had not been martyred in the Circus of Nero, this evidence still would be insufficient to prove that Peter had never been in Rome. The question of his residence in Rome and that of his possible martyrdom and death there are completely distinct. If, on the other hand, it could be proved, which it cannot, that Peter had never been in Rome, then of course, a discussion of his martyrdom and burial in that city would be superfluous.
>
> In view of the meager information which is available at the present time, no certain statement can be made concerning Peter's Roman residence, martyrdom, and burial. One must continually speak in terms of possibilities and probabilities.[4]

The significance of this conclusion lies in the fact that the Catholic Church has constantly claimed that its line of popes can be traced back to Peter as bishop of Rome. In the form of a simple syllogism, the argument would go thus: Peter was the first bishop of Rome; the pope is the bishop of Rome; therefore the pope is the successor of Peter. In response to this argument, we must point out that the Christians of Rome, for the first two centuries, did not elect a successor to Peter but a bishop of Rome. It is impossible to determine how much real ruling power

---

4. *Peter in Rome,* p. 207.

the bishop of Rome had outside of the city itself before the time of Constantine (d. 337).[5] From the time of Constantine onward, Rome was recognized to enjoy the leadership (primacy) over all the other Christian churches, a fact largely—not exclusively—due to Constantine's influence. Therefore, as Rome grew in political primacy as the center of the imperial government, so the ecclesiastical primacy of Rome grew. As Christianity expanded in the first three centuries, the growth of Rome's primacy was necessary to give visible expression of unity in the face of proliferating heresies which were plaguing Christianity. After the fourth century, the primacy of Rome was accepted in the West, i.e. Africa, Italy, parts of northern and western Europe. The primacy no longer depended on Rome as the head of the empire, which ended in the fifth century. After the beginning of the seventh century the bishop of Rome began and directed much of the conversion of the West. This leadership strengthened his power. To complete the picture we may add that in 1054 the Eastern churches broke away from Rome and in the 16th century the Protestant churches of the Reformation followed suit.

Having considered the historical processes by which papal primacy evolved, let us go back and consider the relationship between what the papal office became through history and what Jesus intended Peter's leadership to be. The New Testament describes Peter's leadership as informal and unstructured; decisions were made

---

5. It is interesting to note that the see of Alexandria had authority over its neighboring Egyptian cities before Rome acquired a similar extent of authority over the cities of Italy.

by the apostles as a group, as is seen in Acts, ch. 1-12. It appears that James, not Peter, had the final authority over the Church at Jerusalem. Paul, for his part, took orders from no one, not even from Peter, in his missionary activities.

When we compare this informal leadership of Peter with the absolute leadership exercised by the popes up to the present, we see that the role of the pope has changed markedly from the role Jesus seems to have intended for Peter. Hans Küng points out the paradox in this historical development in the following words: "It is an absurd situation that the Petrine ministry, which was intended, as Catholics in particular see it, to be a rock-like and pastoral ministry, preserving and strengthening the unity of the Church, should have become a gigantic, apparently immovable, inseparable and impassable block of stone barring the way to mutual understanding between the Christian churches" (p. 464).

The "One True Church"

In the days before the second Vatican council it was customary to "prove" that the Roman Catholic Church was the only church founded by Jesus. The proof consisted in showing the Church to possess the four marks of "unity, holiness, catholicity and apostolicity." The air of triumphalism in this approach disenchants more liberal and ecumenically minded theologians. They point to some signs of the Roman church's change on its rigid position as the one true church. One sign is that Vatican II recognizes the Protestant churches as churches.[6] Another

---

6. See the decree on Ecumenism, ch. 1.

sign is that Rome is slowly realizing that it is false to consider Protestant churches as doubtfully Christian, for this is what Rome is officially saying when she claims to be the "one true church." Moreover, some of the disenchantment with the proof of the four marks stems from the new look at apostolic succession—the succession of the popes and bishops—which we shall treat of in the next chapter, "The Hierarchy of the Church."

VII

The Hierarchy
of the Church

Having seen in the preceding chapter that it is necessary to rethink our ideas on the origin of the church of Jesus, we must now consider the origin of the hierarchical *structure* of that Church. Is the present hierarchical structure in accordance with what we find in the New Testament?

We will begin with a description of the various offices which appear in the New Testament—apostles, deacons, deaconesses, teachers, prophets, and presbyters and bishops. Then we shall come to grips with the central issue—the emergence of the office of monarchical bishop. We shall conclude with a brief discussion of the problems of ordination and apostolic succession and the relation between charism and office in the Church.

Apostles

Although disputed by some scholars, it is probable that Jesus himself chose the twelve apostles from among his disciples. After Easter, the expression "The Twelve" became a standard designation for these men. The word *apostle* as used in the New Testament means one who saw the risen Christ and who received a personal commission from him to preach the gospel. It was mainly on the strength of these two qualifications that Paul repeatedly defended himself against his enemies as an apostle in the same sense as were the other "Twelve."[1]

The Greek word *apostolos* is most probably a translation of the Aramaic *selika* meaning "one sent." The change of meaning from this word signifying a temporary function of anyone sent on a mission to a word designating a title of permanent office seems to be original with the New Testament. Another original development in the New Testament regarding the notion of apostle is that the Twelve symbolize in the minds of the Jewish Christians the twelve patriarchs who headed the twelve tribes of Israel in Old Testament times. The expression "twelve apostles" is a symbol of the new leaders who headed the New Israel, the Church, in the New Testament times. To avoid confusion we must add that the broader usage of the term "apostle" in the New Testament includes any Christian missionary such as Barnabas, the cousin and companion of St. Paul. But it was the "Twelve" and Paul who were the foundation of a later evolved line of officials in the Church.[2]

Deacons

According to Acts 6:1-6, the Twelve chose seven men from among their followers or disciples to assist them in the distribution of food to the Greek-speaking widows in Jerusalem. The seven are never called "deacons" and it is

---

1. Cf. Acts 9; Gal 1:11-21.
2. Matthias was later elected to replace the deceased Judas—the first Christians apparently considered it important to keep the number of *twelve* apostles.

disputed whether these seven are deacons as are those in Phil. 1:1 and 1 Tm. 3:8ff. Regardless, the Twelve would be freed to have more time for proclaiming the gospel. Stephen (Acts 6:8ff) and Philip (Acts 8:5), two of these seven, also preached. So the service of distributing food to the needy did not exclude the "deacons" from the service of preaching the gospel. It seems, then, that the deacons in the New Testament had at least two functions, namely, that of assisting in material ministrations and that of preaching. From the second century onward the functions of deacons were more varied and more clearly attested to in various writings.

In Philippians 1:1 Paul addresses the "bishops and deacons" together with the whole church at Philippi. Since in his letter Paul was thanking the Philippians for their material help, it would seem that he addressed those ministers who were chiefly responsible for helping him. Another passage where the word "deacon" is used in the official sense of a minister is 1 Timothy 3:8-13. Here the qualities to be expected of deacons are listed. At times Paul uses the noun "deacon" in a broader sense to mean Paul's helpers in spreading the gospel. Some helpers designated in this manner are Timothy (1 Thes. 3:2), Tychicus and Epaphras.

Scholars have not had much success in finding the prototype of the Christian deacon in the Jewish world, except for a similarity to the *hazzan* who ordinarily assisted the ruler of a Jewish synagogue. There seems to be more similarity in the *Greek* world. Here the term "deacon" meant a servant, messenger, civil official and probably a waiter or menial servant.[3]

---

3. The office of deaconess can only be understood as existing in the New Testament by way of inference. The most probable text is 1

Prophets and Teachers

Prophets and teachers were probably not ordained ministers in the New Testament: "There were in the church at Antioch certain prophets and teachers . . ." (Acts 13:1). These men possessed prophecy and teaching as charisms. The faithful recognized them as inspired by God to carry out a charismatic ministry, i.e. a ministry according to the varied gifts of laymen such as the charisms or special gifts of prophecy (preaching) and teaching. According to Acts 13:1-3, it seems that the church in Antioch was actually led by a group of prophets and teachers who took charge of the liturgical life and directed the missionary activity stemming from Antioch. If this is so, it is not known whether this loose church administration was typical in other Gentile churches in New Testament times. But later, in second century Syria, this custom whereby prophets and teachers substituted for a fixed hierarchy was prevalent.

Presbyters

The English word "presbyter" comes, through the Latin, from the Greek word *presbuteros,* which literally means "older" and is often translated "elder." Although the English word "priest" also comes from the same Greek

---

Timothy 3:11, in which, after the qualities of the deacons are listed, the author adds: "In like manner, let the women be honorable, not slanderers. . . ." These women are not the wives of the deacons, but were deaconesses. The wife of a deacon was not necessarily a deaconess.

term, strictly speaking presbyter is not a synonym for priest, as we shall see.

It seems that the office of presbyter in the New Testament developed from the similar office of presbyter or elder in the Jewish community. This Jewish office of elder existed among the Sanhedrin at Jerusalem and in the local presbyterates commonly found in Jewish communities. Acts 14:22 tells that Paul and Barnabas ordained elders in the churches they founded on their missionary journey in what is now Turkey. It may be concluded from this text and from the letters to Timothy and Titus that it was the customary procedure of the apostles to provide their churches with reliable leaders who would take charge of the churches during their absence and advise them of any problems. The presbyters or elders were chosen from the more experienced and more intelligent members of the community—usually, but not always, the "old" men.

Bishops

In the pagan world of New Testament times the Greek term *episcopos* (i.e. "bishop") was used of men in religious offices (business managers of cult associations) and in secular offices (state and city officials). It is controverted whether the term *episcopos* as used for pagan religious officers influenced the New Testament selection of the term for Christian overseers. The *mebaqqer* is a Hebrew term used in the Dead Sea scrolls for the monarchical leader of a community. It does not seem that the New Testament writers, however, borrowed the idea of the office of the *episcopos* from the writers of the Dead

Sea Scrolls because the office of monarchical bishop does not appear in the New Testament. It appears only after New Testament times.

We may conclude that these two Greek terms *presbuteros* and *episcopos* did not have in New Testament times—in writing other than biblical—the technical meaning which we moderns attach to their English equivalents. Furthermore, a close study of the usage of these two Greek words in the New Testament shows that they were used interchangeably. The best illustration of the use of these two terms as synonyms is found in Paul's speech at Miletus as reported in Acts 20:17 and 28: "From Miletus, however, he (Paul) sent to Ephesus for the presbyters (*presbuterous*) of the church; and when they had come to him and were assembled, he said to them: . . . 'take heed to yourselves and to the whole flock in which the Holy Spirit has placed you as bishops (*episcopous*). . . .' " Note that the speaker uses the two different terms for the same audience. Since there were several bishops, "overseers," in the one community of Ephesus the later monarchical concept of bishop is excluded.[4]

The functions of the Christian presbyter were to celebrate the Holy Eucharist and conduct the liturgical assembly (1 Timothy 2:1-15); to teach and exhort (1 Tm. 6:2); to keep order and administer temporal affairs (Acts 11:30). Regarding the functions of the "bishop" (episcopos), they are not even mentioned in 1 Timothy 3:1-7 or

---

4. These two Greek words are also used interchangeably in the letter to Titus 1:5 and 7; also the variant reading in the first letter of Peter 5:1-2. Other texts which may be cited are Philippians 1:1 and 1 Timothy 3:1-13, but they are not so clear as the three preceding texts.

in Titus 1:7-9. These passages stress the personal qualities of a good "bishop" rather than the duties of his office.

The regular Greek words for priest, *hiereus* and high priest, *archiereus,* were never directly used in the New Testament to mean the ministers of the Church. (Only the author of the epistle to the Hebrews applies the title priest to Christ). In fact, the term seems studiously avoided. The New Testament readers were familiar with this Greek word in a polytheistic or mythological context, because it was the word used for the priests of the pagan religions. One may conjecture that lest the unique priest, Jesus, be associated in any way with these pagan priests, the title *hiereus* was never applied to him or to his ministers. Tertullian and Hippolytus were the first Christian writers to apply the words priest and high priest to ministers in the church.

Origin of Monarchical Episcopacy

Although the modern office of bishop has its origin in the once distinct, eventually combined, offices of *episcopos* and *presbuteros,* there is no monarchical office of bishop before the end of the first century A.D. By monarchical bishop we mean one bishop presiding as the authoritative leader over the entire Christian community in an area. Until at least the end of the first century A.D. the churches were guided by a group of presbyters and/or episcopoi. As late as A.D. 96-98 we find the two terms used interchangeably by Clement of Rome writing to the church at Corinth. (The letter of Clement, of course, is not part of the New Testament.) Monarchical episcopacy probably arose in Asia around A.D. 90 to 100. A clear distinction between episcopos and presbuteros is made by Ignatius of Antioch in his letters written sometime before A.D. 117. Ignatius makes the presbyters and the deacons, subordinate to the bishop. He is also the first clear witness to the "monarchical" episcopate as defined above. Monarchical episcopacy did not begin in Rome until the late second century, and therefore later than in Asia and Syria. We may conclude, therefore, that the office of monarchical bishop did not originate with Jesus or with the apostles: it grew at different times and places out of the need for a greater visible structure.[5]

As a further illustration of the above conclusion, we may observe that the church at Corinth had no leaders (no bishops or elders) but only charismatic Christians. Besides, the church at Antioch was led by prophets and teachers (not bishops or elders).[6] When Paul wrote the letter to the Romans A.D. 57 there were no leaders there (no bishops or elders). In fact, Paul never addresses an appeal to a single official to restore order when needed in a community.

To those who may point to James, the head of the Jerusalem church, (cf. Acts 15) as an example of a New Testament origin of the office of monarchical bishop, scholars reply that James was the head of the Jerusalem church only because he was the closest relative of Jesus. In fact, after his death, Symeon, his closest relative, succeeded

---

5. The first precise dating of a Roman pontificate is that of Pontian, September 28, A.D. 235, the date of his resignation. Furthermore, the first Roman bishop to make an appeal to the precedence of Peter was Stephen I, about A.D. 250.

6. See Acts 11:27 and 13:1-3.

him. If the practice of monepiscopacy had been set down by Jesus for Jerusalem, it would have been followed as a pattern for other cities. It obviously was not.

There have been a number of theories put forth to explain the origin of the monarchical episcopate. The classical theory of the eminent Protestant scholar Lightfoot claims that originally "bishops" and "presbyters" were synonymous terms but that one man from the group of presbyters was finally elevated and nominated a monarchical bishop.

A theory developed by Sohm and Lowrie suggests that originally there was a distinction between the two orders of the presbyter and the bishop. The bishops were "appointed presbyters." They were appointed or ordained to discharge liturgical, pastoral and economic duties in which the deacons helped them. In larger communities there may have been two bishops instead of one. However, according to this theory, the office of bishop was always distinct even as far back as apostolic times. The presbyters held only a position of *honor:* the bishops held a position of ministerial *office.* Gradually the bishops became monarchical, i.e. they began to preside as the authoritative leader of a community. At this stage of development the bishops delegated to the presbyters certain duties or functions (no longer honors) of a liturgical and pastoral nature.

According to Hans Küng, the *episkopoi* were at first concerned only with administrative duties in the Christian community, and therefore they were less highly regarded than the more charismatic ministries of the community. But the first century Christian work, the Didache, puts them on the same level as the other ministers be-

cause they eventually took over other offices as needed:
"The other permanent ministries of the community,
which were 'only' based on a charismatic calling, could
not really compete with the office of *episkopoi* and deacons, which had become institutionalized and was solidly
founded on election by the community" (p. 409). Thus
the *episkopoi* assumed more and more authority, including areas of organization, worship and teaching. "Thus,
while the Church had been founded entirely on the apostles and prophets and in its entirety had inherited the
mantle of the apostles, the *episkopoi* or elders gradually
came to be in a special degree the 'successors of the apostles' within the Church" (p. 409). And before too long,
instead of there continuing to be a number of *episkopoi*
or elders in the community, a monarchical episcopacy
developed. These single bishops became increasingly the
leaders of a wider territory or diocese, rather than of individual local churches.

In *The Office of Apostle in the Early Church,* W.
Schmithals proposes that it was the Jewish Christian
Hegesippus who introduced or at least popularized the
idea of apostolic succession of the monarchical episcopacy. St. Irenaeus expresses well Hegesippus' idea: "Anyone who wishes to see the truth can find in every church
the tradition which the apostles proclaimed in the whole
world and we can enumerate the bishops of the various
churches installed by the apostles, as well as their successors down to the present day" (Ireneaus III, 3.1.).[7]

---

7. Note that this opinion of Ireneaus is by no means capable of being
   substantiated, though it has been accepted without question by
   generations of Catholics.

From the end of the second century the theory of the apostolic succession of bishops was never again fundamentally called into question within the Church until recently.

Hans Küng asserts that the important point is not to prove an *historical* connection or link of a Church structure with Jesus, but an *existential* link, i.e. the important point is whether or not the Church received Jesus' message in faith and lives it convincingly (cf. p. 79). A popular news magazine accurately reported the current thought of many Catholic scholars: "Apostolic succession is now seen by many Catholic theologians as a continuity of doctrine and Christian commitment from one generation to another within the church community—not as a sort of ecclesiastical relay race, with the baton passing from bishop to bishop."[8]

Though we have touched upon the problem of apostolic succession above, particularly in the relation to the evolution of the monarchical episcopacy, it needs some further development along with the related question of ordination. What do we know of the way in which the apostles passed on their office to their successors and delegates? Today this handing on of the office is done by the sacrament of ordination. Does this practice originate in apostolic times?

There is no clear-cut evidence in the New Testament and other early writings which answers these questions clearly. It seems that the apostles, the presbyter-bishops

---

8. *Time,* May 25, 1970, p. 76.

and the deacons were the leaders of the primitive church. But there were also "delegates" of the apostles such as Timothy and Titus.

Whether or not Paul wrote the pastoral epistles to Timothy and Titus, these letters offer several peculiarities about some men who seemed to have been delegated in a special manner by the apostles. One peculiarity is that Timothy at Ephesus and Titus at Crete are not permanently attached to these places. They are not even attached to a specific local church in Ephesus or Crete. Besides, the apostolic delegates do not rule in a particular community in Ephesus or in Crete but each delegate supervises several communities and the presbyter-bishops within these communities. These men can be reprimanded by the delegate. At least we surmise this authority from such texts as 1 Timothy 5:19-20: "Do not listen to an accusation against a presbyter unless it is supported by two or three witnesses."

This text tells us that the internal unity of a community is assured by a college of presbyter-bishops. We see this, furthermore from such saying as: ". . . Set right anything that is defective and . . . appoint (or ordain?) presbyters in every city" (Titus 1:5). It appears that Titus was going around and ordaining presbyters in each community and that the college of presbyters, not Titus, ruled the community. From the same text it appears that in this college of presbyters no one individual has the fullness of apostolic power to ordain other presbyters. Apparently only the apostles and their delegates had this power. This is further borne out in Acts 14:23: "They (Paul and Barnabas) had appointed (or ordained?) presbyters for them (for the disciples of Lystra, Iconium and Antioch) in each church. . . ."

What, then, is the relationship of these delegates of the apostles to the rest of the church leaders or members of "the hierarchy" in the primitive church? The delegates shared the power of the apostles to appoint presbyters; and, like later bishops, they were overseers of communities. On the other hand, these delegates—as delegates—had less authority than the apostles. However, it must be admitted that the above texts are not cogent in showing the sacramental ordination and succession of ministers to the order of priesthood.

Conclusion—Ministry

The foregoing historical study illustrates that the tightly structured hierarchical arrangement of the Church's ministry as it exists today cannot be considered scriptural in its origins. The orders of ministers that developed in the New Testament church evolved from the needs of the church in the circumstances of its life at that time. If we were to carry this story further into the middle ages, we would see that what was originally a purely pragmatic development solidified, into a structure that was legitimated by a carefully worked out doctrinal apology. We may ask whether the Church might not have much to gain by a return to the primitive church's greater emphasis on charismatic leadership rather than ministerial leadership.

VIII

Did Jesus Forbid Remarriage?

Of all the problems related to Christian moral teaching, one of the most sensitive is the problem of divorce. The Catholic Church's adamant prohibition of divorce is unequivocally stated in Canon Law: A marriage which is ratified and consummated cannot be dissolved except by death itself (Canon 1118). This prohibition is based on the words of Jesus in the Gospels, which we shall quote below. The Roman Church has traditionally considered the words of Jesus regarding divorce and remarriage as having the binding force of law and therefore absolutely forbidding divorce and remarriage. The Church has considered unjustifiable the allowance of divorce and remarriage by other Christian churches.

In recent years this strict teaching has been challenged by thinkers within the Church. Scripture scholars in America have been grappling with the problem from the biblical point of view. Some continue to defend the prevailing position that Jesus absolutely prohibited divorce and remarriage, but some are proposing a new interpretation of the pertinent biblical passages.

We shall consider both these interpretations, some historical aspects of the indissolubility of marriage and the current status of the problem of divorce.

New Testament Texts on Divorce

Since we shall refer frequently to the New Testament passages concerning divorce in the following discussion, these texts are quoted in full below:

MATTHEW 5:31-32:   It was also said, "Whenever a man divorces his wife, he must give her a decree of divorce." What I say to you is: everyone who divorces his wife—lewd conduct is a separate case—forces her to commit adultery. The man who marries a divorced woman likewise commits adultery.

MATTHEW 19:3-9:   Some Pharisees came up to him and said, to test him, "May a man divorce his wife for any reason whatever?" He replied, "Have you not read that at the beginning the Creator made them male and female and declared, 'For this reason a man shall leave his father and mother and cling to his wife, and the two shall become as one'? Thus they are no longer two but one flesh. Therefore, let no man separate what God has joined." They said to him, "Then why did Moses command divorce and the promulgation of a divorce decree?" "Because of your stubbornness Moses let you divorce your wives," he replied; "but at the beginning it was not that way. I now say to you, whoever divorces his wife (lewd conduct is a separate case) and marries another commits adultery, and the man who marries a divorced woman commits adultery."

MARK 10:11-12:   He told them, "Whoever divorces his wife and marries another commits adultery against her;

and the woman who divorces her husband and marries another commits adultery."

LUKE 16:18: Everyone who divorces his wife and marries another commits adultery. The man who marries a woman divorced from her husband likewise commits adultery.

1 CORINTHIANS 7:12-16: As for the other matters, although I know of nothing the Lord has said, I say: If any brother has a wife who is an unbeliever but is willing to live with him, he must not divorce her. And if any woman has a husband who is an unbeliever but is willing to live with her, she must not divorce him. The unbelieving husband is consecrated by his believing wife; the unbelieving wife is consecrated by her believing husband. If it were otherwise, your children should be unclean; but as it is, they are holy.

If the unbeliever wishes to separate, however, let him do so. The believing husband or wife is not bound in such cases. God has called you to live in peace. Wife, how do you know that you will not save your husband; or you, husband, that you will not save your wife?

Interpretation of These Texts

As stated above, the Church has traditionally interpreted the words of Jesus in the Gospel (quoted above) as a definitive prohibition of divorce and remarriage. The exceptions to this "law" given by Matthew and Paul represent "difficulties" to be harmonized with this absolute prohibition: "Most scholars admit that Christ himself admitted no exceptions, though the phrase 'except for fornication,' found in both of Matthew's passages, presents some difficulties."[1]

---

1. *New Catholic Encyclopedia,* "Divorce," vol. 4, p. 930.

The new interpretation understands the words of Jesus on divorce as an *ideal,* rather than as a law.[2]

Many of Jesus' moral and ethical teachings were collected and presented as the "Sermon on the Mount" in the Gospel of Matthew. The prohibition of divorce quoted above is among these sayings. Biblical scholars generally agree that the teachings presented in this "Sermon" are to be regarded as *ideals* of Christian conduct, rather than as laws. In fact, one of Jesus' main purposes in his moral teaching was to break the bonds of legalism with which faithful Jews had been tied to the observance of the Old Testament laws.[3] The Sermon presents a set of attitudes

---

2. One example of the new interpretation through the use of form criticism is as follows: There are five steps in the literary history of the four texts which in turn involve two events, namely, the development of an isolated saying whose time and place is completely lost, and its integration into the development of another pericope, that of Christ's debate with the authorities (Mt. 19:3-9). These are the five steps. Mt. 5:31-32 represents the earliest statement of Christ's saying. The second state in the development of this saying is found in Luke 16:18: "Everyone who puts away his wife and marries another commits adultery; and he who marries a woman who has been put away from her husband commits adultery." The third state in the process of development is in Mark 10:11-12: "And he said to them, 'Whoever puts away his wife and marries another, commits adultery against her; and if the wife puts away her husband, and marries another, she commits adultery.' " The fourth stage is seen in the appendage of Mark 10:11-12 to Mark 10:2-9. The last step is the transition of Mark 10:2-9 into Matthew 19:3-9 and the complete integration of the saying as found in its second stage (Luke 16-18) into that newly phrased debate of Matthew 19:3-9. D. Crossan, "Divorce and Remarriage in the New Testament," p. 12 in *The Bond of Marriage,* ed. W. W. Bassett, University of Notre Dame Press, South Bend, Ind., 1968.

3. Cf. for example, Mt. 12:9-14, where Jesus cures the man with a shriveled hand and the Pharisees object asking: "Is it lawful to work a cure on the Sabbath?"

which Christians are to hold relative to what is right and wrong in conduct. The Church has never interpreted the other moral principles contained in this sermon as having the strict binding force of law. Some examples will bear this out.

If interpreted literally, Matthew 5:33-37 would prohibit all taking of oaths: "You have heard the commandment imposed on your forefathers, 'Do not take a false oath; rather, make good to the Lord all your pledges.' What I tell you is: do not swear at all. Do not swear by heaven (it is God's throne), nor by the earth (it is his footstool), nor by Jerusalem (it is the city of the great King); do not swear by your head (you cannot make a single hair white or black). Say, 'Yes' when you mean 'Yes' and 'No' when you mean 'No.' Anything beyond that is from the evil one." It seems that these words mean that the Christian must simply say yes when he means yes and no when he means no. He must be so honest in speech that no oath is necessary. Yet it does not take a detailed historical study of the tradition of the Church to learn that she has never forbidden the taking of oaths. In fact, she has on occasion legislated to require the taking of oaths.[4] This legislation is not only far from the ideal proposed by Jesus but seems directly opposed to it.

Another example is the words of Jesus on nonviolence: "You have heard that it was said: 'an eye for an eye' and 'a tooth for a tooth.' But I say to you not to resist the evildoer; on the contrary, if someone strike you on the right

---

4. For example, until recently, each major seminary professor has had to take an oath against "modernism" at the beginning of every academic year.

cheek, turn to him the other also; and if anyone would go to law with you and take your tunic, let him take your cloak as well; and whoever forces you to go for one mile, go with him two. To him who asks you, give; and from him who would borrow of you, do not turn away" (Mt. 5:38-42). The Church has certainly never in her history understood or followed these words literally (witness the many "Holy Wars" she has encouraged throughout her history). It is a strange paradox that the Church has, in fact, seemed to prefer the risk of war to the granting of a single divorce-remarriage!

Simply reading through the Sermon on the Mount will show many other examples of ethical teaching of Jesus that have never been considered as laws.[5]

Thus we can conclude that Jesus' prohibition of divorce must not be looked upon as a stricter law to replace a more lenient Old Testament law. His words were certainly not intended by him as proof texts from which the later Church could decide how to legislate regarding divorce and remarriage. However, just because the teachings of Jesus present ideals rather than laws, we cannot conclude that these may be taken lightly. On the contrary, the Sermon on the Mount makes it clear that adopting the attitudes contained in it is to effect a complete change in the life of the Christian. These attitudes are not options, but are rather dynamic norms of conduct which demand persistent and serious effort. Therefore, it does not follow from this new interpretation of the New Testament texts that divorce may be obtained for any light reason.

---

5. For more examples in addition to the above, cf. Donald W. Shaner, *A Christian View of Divorce According to the Teaching of the New Testament,* E. J. Brill, Leiden, Netherlands, 1969.

Before concluding this discussion of the new interpretation, we must say a word about the exception clauses in Matthew (i.e. "everyone who divorces his wife—lewd conduct is a separate case" . . . 5:32; cf. 19:9). While these clauses are found in the original Greek text, most Protestant and Catholic biblical scholars agree that they were inserted by Matthew and are not the words of Jesus. This fact does not, however, lessen their authority, for they still constitute a part of God's inspired word. But the problem of seeking out their meaning remains. In recent years there have been many different interpretations made of these clauses, but scholars do not agree on any of these interpretations.

The opinon of J. Bonsirven is attractive. He concludes after a close scrutiny of all the Rabbinic material (Tobit 8:9; Sirach 23:22-23; the Talmud, the Mischna, etc.) that marriages which were illegitimate according to the prescriptions of Lv. 18:7-8, i.e. incestuous unions, were called in Hebrew *zenuth*. This word was translated into Greek by *porneia*. Acts 15:20 favors Bonsirven's view. Verse 20 lists practices to be observed by Gentile converts. Among other things they are to abstain from *porneia*.

What is the meaning of *porneia?* Bonsirven answers that there is a striking similarity between the abstention from *porneia* in Acts 15:20 and the injunctions of Leviticus which were intended for both Jew and non-Jew as in Acts 15:20. One of the injunctions of Leviticus was incestuous unions. Hence, inasmuch as the abstentions or injunctions of Acts 15:20 seemed based on the regulations of Leviticus 17-18, it also seems that the *porneia* of Acts 15:20 regards as illegal those unions that are incestuous and of a concubinage nature. Consequently, Bersirven would incorporate his theory in the following paraphrase of Matthew's clauses thus: "No one is allowed to dismiss his wife—except because of an invalid marriage, on grounds of incest, concubinage—and if he remarries, he commits adultery." Moreover, the incestuous union called *porneia* in 1 Cor. 5:1 supports the view of Bonsirven.

Regardless of which is the best interpretation, however, it is clear that these clauses represent an early Christian adaptation of the Lord's saying to fit a situation not originally foreseen.

In the above exposition of the more recent interpretation of the New Testament teaching on divorce and remarriage, we have seen that Jesus proposed as an ideal the indissolubility of marriage. However, Matthew and Paul added exceptions or adaptations to Jesus' teachings. Matthew's exception clauses reflect the thinking of the community of his era, which found itself faced with the problem of pagans married against the laws of Leviticus 18 (presuming that the above interpretation of Bonsirven is correct) and wishing to be baptized and live in marriage with Christian Jews. The Christian community solved this problem by allowing divorce and remarriage. Paul was confronted with a different problem (cf. 1 Cor 7:12-16). To couples who could no longer live in peace after one party became a Christian, Paul allowed divorce. The Church later extended Paul's interpretation from divorce to remarriage. This is a good example of how the Church uses her power well in extending the permission granted by Paul in what is known as the "Pauline privilege." A consideration of these two exceptions by Matthew and Paul made so early in the history of Christianity is very important for a fruitful reevaluation of the

Church's adamant prohibition of divorce. If there were already two exceptions or adaptations to Jesus' teaching made in response to different life-situations within the brief span of New Testament times, how many more adaptations ought to be considered now? The whole Church, the hierarchy and the Christian communities must confront the problems in which they must reconcile the unqualified condemnation of divorce and remarriage by the Church with the call of God, who "has called us to peace" (1 Cor 7:15).

Historical Aspects of the Indissolubility of Marriage

In recent years several serious studies have been made tracing the history of the Church's dispensations of marriages which had been ratified and consummated. Leaving aside the knotty problem of what precisely constitutes the essence of the marriage bond (the consent of both parties? the consummation? both?), it is clear that the general practice of the Church has been to deny permission for divorce and remarriage to Christians whose marriage had been ratified and consummated. Nevertheless, despite the fact that the granting of such permission has been rare, the Church has used the power to do so. If the Church has this power and has used it in the past, why cannot she use it more frequently in the complex situations of modern life?[6]

---

6. It seems like hair-splitting to enlarge upon the subtle problem in history of a divorce being granted only by a local Church and not by the universal church and also the question as to whether, in those cases in which the Church did grant a divorce, the original marriage was a true marriage in the first place.

We will offer here the conclusions of three of these studies on the historical question of the indissolubility of marriage.[7] The first is by H. Crouzel, S.J.[8] who states: "Between the second and fourth centuries and the beginning of the fifth century, there is only one text (that of Ambrosiaster, the work of an unknown writer attributed to St. Ambrose of Milan) which clearly professes the legitimacy of a second marriage of the husband after repudiation of an adulterous wife." A. J. Bevilacqua, who has carried a study through the entire first millennium of Christianity, likewise concludes to only rare examples of true cases of divorce and remarriage.[9] But the fact that he does find some, no matter how few, does support the view that the Church has used this power in the past, and therefore could use it now if she deemed it necessary.

The second conclusion is by M. Hurley, S.J.:[10]

Since Trent the absolute indissolubility of consummated sacramental marriage, *i.e.,* its indissolubility even in case of adultery, has continued to be the clear, certain authoritative teaching of the Roman Catholic Church. It appears as such in, for instance, the encyclical *Casti Connubii* of Pius XI and more recently in the *Pastoral Constitution on the Church in the Modern World* of the Second Vatican Council. But the precise relationship between this Church doctrine and the Christian revelation is neither defined by

---

7. These two studies are not necessarily the most comprehensive, but they suffice for our purpose.
8. "Séparation ou remarriage selon les Péres anciens," *Gregorianum,* 1966, p. 492.
9. cf. *Proceedings of the Catholic Theological Society of America,* 1967, pp. 253-306.
10. *The Irish Theological Quarterly,* 1968, p. 65.

authority nor clear in itself. The Roman Catholic Church does hold this doctrine and does formally propose it to its members but it does not formally propose it to us as revealed truth precisely. And so at the fourth session of Vatican II Archbishop Zoghby could suggest that the Church might change her attitude toward divorce. In other words the indissolubility of consummated sacramental marriage even in case of adultery is not a dogma.

From the foregoing conclusions, we note two important points. First, the Church has only rarely dissolved a sacramental Christian marriage and allowed remarriage. But this rarity suffices to show that she can dissolve more sacramental Christian marriages if she judges fit to do so. It also shows that although she cannot say for certain what constitutes the essence of marriage she can nevertheless dissolve them. Second, the authoritative teaching and practice of the Church, however strict it may be, does not fall under her *dogmatic* teaching authority. So, for example, she has never defined the meaning of the exceptive clauses in Matthew 5:32 and 19:9.

The Status of the Problem of Divorce Today

In consideration of the foregoing discussion, we may conceive of the possibility of a change in the Church's position on divorce in the future. Perhaps the Church will read the handwriting on the wall and grant permission for divorce and remarriage not only in the cases of adultery and desertion but in the less easily defined equally serious cases such as real psychological incompatibility. Dr. J. D. Sullivan supports the idea of marriage as indissoluble, yet makes a statement requiring serious reflection:

Yet I knew deeply and basically that there are hundreds of thousands and, perhaps, millions of people who, in view of the existing social attitudes and in view of the sanctions operative in society and operative among their friends and relatives, are in reality incompatible of so relating exclusively, permanently and in proximity. Again, I cannot prove this to you except to appeal to the fact that there are indications from the general statistics of the country, including Catholics, that this is the case.[11]

We might even consider that the increasing divorce rate among Catholics is an indication of the voice of the Holy Spirit. Through the intolerable sufferings ending in divorce for many sincere Catholics, perhaps the Spirit is trying to tell the Church that God never intended this suffering. Post-Vatican II theology urges theologians and the hierarchy to listen to the Spirit speaking through the voice of the laity. Perhaps the experience of the laity, in living the teaching on divorce as traditionally understood, is a sign that the Church has been too limited in her interpretation of Jesus' teaching. In this connection the objection that the common good is at stake ought to be reconsidered, for the common good embraces all, including a married couple in an intolerable situation. It is not necessarily true, either, that the more frequent granting of divorce is going to open the floodgates of many new evils.

However, we must never lose sight of the ideal proposed by Jesus that marriage *is* a permanent bond. If the Church does relax somewhat her position on divorce, she must at the same time stress the ideal of Jesus, and also

---

11. *Proceedings of the Catholic Theological Society of America,* 1967, p. 250.

emphasize the teaching of Paul on married love: "Husbands, love your wives, just as Christ loved the Church and delivered himself up for her. . . . Even thus ought husbands also to love their wives as their own bodies. He who loves his own wife, loves himself . . . and let the wife respect her husband" (Eph. 5:25-33).

IX

Did Jesus Resurrect?

The resurrection of Jesus is one of the central doctrines of Christianity, for as Paul says, if he is not risen, our faith is in vain (1 Cor. 15:14). For the past decade the presses have been rolling out an abundance of literature on the theology of the resurrection; and the problems related to this pivotal doctrine are the concern of people in all Christian denominations. There are three main approaches taken in the present-day discussion: The meaning of the resurrection is sought first in its relationship to the crucifixion (R. Bultmann, K. Barth). Second, in the exact words and deeds of the historical Jesus (W. Marxsen, G. Ebeling); third, in its relationship to the expectation of the general resurrection and the judgment at the end of the world (U. Wilckens, W. Pannenberg).[1] The present chapter is confined to the second approach, and

---

1. The German works of the scholars advocating these three main approaches may be found on pages 106ff of Moule's book listed below.

is an attempt to answer the question of what we can know of Christ's resurrection through history, i.e. through rational biblical interpretation, rather than through faith. Of all the questions surrounding the resurrection, this seems the most crucial.

We shall begin with a consideration of Marxsen's theory on the resurrection. This important Protestant scholar first published his article in German in 1964[2] and it was published in English in 1968.[3] This article raised the discussion of the resurrection to a new level in the German scholarly world but it has not yet made its impact on the English speaking world.

What We Can Know of Christ's Resurrection from History

Marxsen begins by pointing out that an event is not to be considered historical simply because the biblical writers and the first Christians *believed* that it was historical. Rather, we must test the reliability of their historical judgments. The evangelists, Paul and the early Christians *believed* that Jesus resurrected bodily and they preached this as a fact. But this is not historical proof to us in the twentieth century that Jesus rose bodily.

There are two alleged facts that we must contend with: the empty tomb and the appearance of Jesus. There have

---

2. Marxsen, W., *Die Auferstehung Jesu als historisches und als theologisches Problem* (Gutersloh, 1964).
3. *The Significance of the Message of the Resurrection for Faith in Jesus Christ,* ed. by C. F. D. Moule, Naperville, Illinois, Allenson, Inc.

been a number of unsuccessful historical attempts to prove that the tomb of Jesus *was* empty on Easter morning. But even if it could be proven historically, there can be different interpretations of the fact: the tomb was empty because the disciples removed the corpse (Mt. 27:64) or else Jesus was actually risen.

Mark 16:1-6 contains the earliest version of the story of the empty tomb. Let us suppose that this story is meant to convey a fact of history. What does it recount? The women say that they saw an empty tomb. This is an "historical" statement, i.e. it is not based on their faith. Therefore, when we of the twentieth century accept this statement, we are not making an act of faith but are merely trusting the correct judgment of these women. Thus we can at least reach back in time to an empty tomb.

But the question must be raised whether the earliest story of the empty tomb is in fact intended to be an historical account, or whether it was a particular form in which the resurrection was preached. Marxsen holds this second alternative. It is obvious that in either case no satisfactory historical proof that the tomb was empty can be put forth.

Similar problems arise in regard to the appearance of Jesus to his apostles and to other disciples. There are two traditions present in the stories of these appearances. In the first group of biblical texts, only the *fact* of the appearances is mentioned: the simple claim by certain witnesses to have seen the crucified Christ. In the second group, elaborate tales of the appearances are found, especially in the Gospels. For example, Jesus speaks, eats, passes through a closed door (e.g. Luke 24). This group of stories represents a literary development over the first group.[4]

What was the *manner* of this seeing of Jesus? We can only ascertain how the seeing has been described. The key Greek word (*ophthe*) in these accounts of the appearances may be translated in two ways: Jesus *was seen,* e.g. by Peter (the activity being on the part of the witnesses); Jesus *appeared* or let himself be seen (the action is initiated by Jesus, i.e., *he* appeared). Marxsen concludes that it is hardly possible to establish the precise meaning from the Greek form of the word.

There are two hypotheses to explain the manner of this seeing: a "subjective vision" and an "objective vision." In the case of the "subjective vision," the vision is a *result* of the witnesses' faith.

They saw Jesus *because* they believed him to be risen. In other words, the vision took place only within the minds of those who believed Jesus to be risen even though they may have claimed an *objective* vision.

If the vision were an "objective vision," it was still the result of the witnesses' faith, even though this time it is something which occurred outside their minds. In either case, the faith of the witnesses created a vision, whether the vision was subjective or objective. Marxsen concludes that the resurrection of Jesus cannot be historically proven because all we have is a description by witnesses who claim that they saw Jesus risen: "In historical terms it can only be established, though quite reliably, that witnesses, after the death of Jesus, claimed that some-

---

4. "Scholars have no doubt at all that the first group is older in terms of the history of the tradition," Marxsen, op. cit., p. 26.

5. Op. cit., p. 31.

thing had happened to them which they described as seeing Jesus, and reflection on this experience led them to the *interpretation* that Jesus had been raised from the dead."[5] In Marxsen's view, the reason why the witnesses of the appearances made the interpretation that Jesus had risen from the dead was the Jewish notion that at the end of the world there would be a general resurrection. Since they thought they saw Jesus, they concluded that he was raised from the dead and that the general resurrection had already begun in the case of Jesus.

Another belief followed on the disciples' belief that Jesus was alive, namely that a community or church was formed by him and that they were commissioned to preach the risen Christ and his church. In 1 Cor. 9:1, for example, Paul appeals to the appearance of Jesus after his crucifixion as evidence for his appointment as an apostle: "Am I not an apostle? Have I not seen Jesus our Lord?" Paul is not alone in tracing his mission to his vision of Jesus. In the conclusion of Matthew's Gospel (28:16ff), the appearance is connected with the mission expressed in the command: "Go therefore and make disciples of all nations. . . ." In John 20:19-23, the mission to forgive and retain sins is based upon the appearance of Jesus. The same holds for Acts 10:40-42, where Jesus' appearance is the reason for the witnesses' mission of preaching. Thus we have seen that the witnesses of the appearances of the risen Jesus draw two conclusions: that he was risen from the dead and that he gave them a mission to preach him and his Church.[6]

---

6. The scholars we are concerned with are not very concerned with the well-known discrepancies in the accounts of the appearances.

Critique of Marxsen's Thesis

Perhaps the greatest merit of Marxsen's approach is the clarity with which the historical method is applied. He throws much light on the problem relating to where history ends and faith begins. He shows how far a person like himself can go, who does not believe in the bodily resurrection of Jesus. He thereby tacitly leaves the burden on the shoulders of the believer to say where precisely his faith begins and history ends. One may simply dismiss Marxsen as a skeptic but one must admit that he is a learned skeptic who has applied the historical method with a great degree of sophistication.

Marxsen's essay truly presents a most challenging position because of its coherence and subtlety. When Catholic systematic theologians and biblical scholars seriously take up some of his implications, a fruitful dialogue will ensue. Marxsen's ingenious attack on the corporeal resurrection of Jesus may prove to be the most far-reaching since the comparative religion assault of S. Reinach's *Orpheus* in 1909. It would reveal a misunderstanding of Marxsen's position to "refute" him with passages in which the evangelists and Paul say clearly that the Jesus who was crucified really rose from the tomb. If one were to point out to Marxsen Paul's claim to have received his revelation from Jesus (Gal. 1:12), or Paul's enumeration

---

They presume them to constitute an unsolved problem. Incidentally, it would be unacceptable scholarship to deny all historical validity to the appearance narratives solely on the basis of their inconsistencies.

of those who had seen Jesus risen (1 Cor. 15:5-8), Marxsen would reply that Paul and others honestly *thought* they saw Jesus bodily risen.

We will point out three objections to Marxsen's thesis. First, he holds the view that the accounts of the appearances are not meant to be historical, but are rather a "particular form in which the resurrection was preached" (p. 25). He does not explain and substantiate this assertion. And this is understandable, since with his approach it would be very difficult to explain the appearances of Jesus. But it is just as unscientific to have recourse to another explanation because one does not understand the appearances as it is to hold the view of objective appearances even though one cannot explain the nature of these appearances. But perhaps Marxsen asserts his view because of his supposition that the dead do not rise. If so, then he has already prejudged that Jesus also did not rise.

Second, Marxsen does not account for the origin of the narratives of the appearances. It is certain that the furthest thing from the minds of Jesus' followers was that he was alive. In addition, it is very difficult to understand the power of the belief that Jesus was risen—enough power to result in the formation of a church or community around this belief—if there were not objective reality behind these claimed appearances. In a critique of Marxsen's essay, U. Wilckens, a Protestant biblical scholar, writes: "And precisely because it is quite impossible that disciples of Jesus should have reacted to the catastrophe of his death by the conviction suddenly dawning upon them that he had been raised from the dead—which had never previously been asserted in Israel of any mortal—

the so-called hypothesis of the subjective vision must be excluded as an explanation".[7]

Third, it seems that Marxsen could carry the historical method back another step in time. He contends that history can only lead the twentieth century Christian back to a *claim* of witnesses that Jesus rose, and that it is only by faith that the Christian can reach back to the event itself of God's action in raising Jesus. The consideration which Marxsen omits is the transformation of the disciples from timid and fearful men to courageous preachers of the word. Undoubtedly, before the resurrection the disciples were stunned, frightened and disillusioned. The death of Jesus placed the severest stress on their faith in him as the Messiah. This stress is expressed in the words of the disciples en route to Emmaus: "But we *had* hoped that he was the one to redeem Israel" (Luke 24:21). It seems then that something happened *to* them (an objective appearance of Jesus) not merely in them (subjective vision). In other words, it is hard to maintain that this transformation was the result of merely an occurrence within the minds of the witnesses.

The Mode of Christ's Risen Body

Having considered the relationship between history and faith in the fact of the resurrection, let us go now to the problem of the kind of body which the risen Christ had. In this area, the discussion among scholars has progressed beyond such theories as these: Jesus did not die but was merely in a coma; the appearances were a fraud invented

---

7. Moule, *op. cit.*, p. 61.

by the apostles; the appearances were a sort of group hallucination; the early Christians were influenced by pagan legends and mystery cults about dying and rising gods.

There are a number of theories as to the manner of the resurrection and the body of the risen Jesus. The "physical recomposition theory" was taught through the middle ages and is still popular, though not among critical theologians. This idea considered Jesus' resurrection to be the same kind of occurrence as the raising of Jairus' daughter (Mark 5:22ff) or the widow's son. (Luke 7:11). But scholars have moved on from this belief that the original physical body of Christ was raised to more sophisticated theories.

The "psychical-research" theory holds that the soul of Jesus, through the will of God, assumed a phantom-body of the "astral" or "ectoplasmic" kind in order to appear to the disciples while the crucified body remained in the tomb. There would be some kind of objectivity to the appearance of this body. However, it is scientifically debatable whether such a body may even be called a temporary phenomenon. Besides, this theory does not explain the scriptural references to the empty tomb. Catholic theologians find such a theory unacceptable.

Another explanation holds that the soul of a human being contains within itself the power to create its own risen body.[8] I doubt that science has advanced sufficiently to warrant such a view. On the other hand, nobody knows the ultimate possible limits of the achieve-

---

8. It is unclear whether the Catholic Swiss theologian, Max Brändle, accepts this theory. See *Theology Digest* volume 16, 1968, p. 19.

ments of science. And nobody knows the ultimate possibilities of Christ's human nature or simply of human nature! Would it be too daring to suggest that if science were to show this theory possible, it would be compatible with the dogma of Jesus' resurrection and the general resurrection at the end of the world? Although the problem is scientific rather than biblical, nothing in Scripture seems to exclude the possibility.

The "eschatological-body" theory presupposes that what gives a body identity is not the material of which it is composed, but the identity of the soul to which it belongs. According to this theory, Christ's risen body may be a model of what our risen bodies will be at the end of time. If so, then what is said of the qualities of his risen body (cf. 1 Cor. 15:42-44, 52-54) applies to our future risen bodies, and what applies to the latter applies to his risen body. The glorified risen bodies at the end of the world will have the same qualities as the glorified body of Jesus. If our risen bodies will be like his, his was then like ours will be. If our risen bodies will not need the material of our mortal bodies as seems evident from the fact that after death the body decays in the ground, perhaps the risen body of Jesus likewise had no need of the actual body that had been crucified. If so, while Jesus appeared or was eating with the apostles and showing them his wounds, the discarded mortal body was still lying in the tomb.

There are a number of difficulties involved in the above theory. For one, it does not account for the empty tomb. For another, the assumptions about the condition of "risen" or glorified bodies are pure speculation and take no account of the fact that we actually have no knowledge of what will be the manner of the general resurrection and the mode of the body in that state. In addition, it is based upon a dualistic body-soul dichotomizing of man which was not part of the Jewish mentality at the time of the apostles.

A closely related but more acceptable theory holds that the soul of Jesus was reunited to his body in some unknown manner. His body was not only revivified but transformed.[9] That is, the body of Jesus assumed its bodily way of living in a true human body but the body was transformed by God. Jesus rose to a new kind of life, not limited by matter, time, space. Jesus' risen body existed very differently from that of the widow's son (Luke 7:11), who resumed life as before, i.e., limited by time and space and destined to die again.

This explanation fits in well with the fact that the risen Jesus was not immediately recognized by the Gospel witnesses. In spite of their initial failure to recognize him, the transformed Jesus is still Jesus! Paul speaks of the general resurrection in this manner: "So is it with the resurrection of the dead. What is sown in the earth is subject to decay, what rises is incorruptible. What is sown is ignoble, what rises is glorious. Weakness is sown, strength rises up. A natural body is put down and a spiritual body comes up. If there is a natural body, be sure there is also a spiritual body" (1 Cor. 15:42-44). This theory agrees well with both the biblical references to the empty tomb and to the appearances to the witnesses as objective appearances. This is an acceptable theory.

---

9. Cf. W. Pannenberg in "Did Jesus Really Rise From the Dead?" *Dialog* 4 (1965) 128-135.

The last theory is that of the completely *spiritual* or *symbolic resurrection* with no bodily resurrection occurring at all.[10] The biblical narratives of the resurrection are all symbolic ways of speaking about Jesus' victory over death, his glorification and spiritual happiness. The general argument for this theory is that bodily resurrection was the only way in which the Jewish mind could understand life after death. To the Jewish mind, bodily resurrection was the only way of stressing the continuity and the identity between the body laid in the tomb and the person who was known to be alive afterwards.

The theory of a symbolic resurrection does not account for the empty tomb. Also, such a theory is difficult to reconcile with the Church's theologically traditional teaching that Jesus rose bodily. At the same time, it cannot be denied that there are biblical passages which can easily be used to defend the spiritual or symbolic resurrection theory.[11]

The Resurrection as an Historical Event

Another current debate among scholars concerns the extent to which one may speak of the resurrection of Jesus

10. Cf. H. Grass, *Ostergeschehen und Osterberichte,* 2nd ed.; Göttingen, 1962.
11. I do not take seriously the alleged words of E. Schillebeeckx quoted in *Time,* Oct. 4, 1968, p. 58, until I can find them in his writings: "The resurrection, he suggests, does not imply the physical recomposition of Jesus' body but 'the impact of his personality on his disciples and his presence in the hearts of all Christians.'" We might mention for those concerned about Christ's divinity that even if the theory of spiritual resurrection were proven true, the doctrine of Christ's divinity would not be thereby assailed.

as an "historical" event. Some assert that an event may be called historical when it is synonymous with "what has happened."[12] Pannenberg argues that precisely because the risen Jesus became known at a definite time, in a limited number of events and to a particular number of men, we should call the resurrection an historical event.

Other scholars, attempting to be more precise, assert that in order that an event be considered historical, it must occur in our space-time continuum—it must be localizable in space and datable in time. There are two schools of thought within the scope of this opinion. One holds that the resurrection qualified as an event in time (sometime in the 30's A.D.) but not in space. The actual occurrence of the resurrection of Jesus was such that no human witness could have seen anything happen (in space) had he been present. Therefore, Christ's resurrection is only questionably considered an historical event.

The other school of thought is exemplified by G. G. O'Collins, "The resurrection is not an event in space and time and hence should not be called historical." In his view, all that went on before Jesus rose into a glorified body is historical (i.e., localized in time and space); but after the resurrection events cannot be considered historical because Jesus was in his glorified existence. O'Collins then applies his definition of what can be called "historical" to the appearances of Jesus: "These appearances are historical from the side of those who encountered the

---

12. G. G. O'Collins, S.J., ascribes this opinion to W. Pannenberg and G. W. H. Lamp in "Is the Resurrection an Historical Event?" *Heythrop Journal*, vol. 8 (1967) 381-387.

risen Lord, but not from the side of Christ himself. These episodes do not occur at a certain time and place in his risen life. His glorified existence is not localizable and datable for the historian . . . the appearances of the risen Jesus are not historical from his side, even if they do form part of the history of Peter, Paul and the other witnesses of the risen Lord."[13]

O'Collins' criterion of what constitutes an historical event is acceptable enough, but even using this criterion we may consider the resurrection an historical event. While it is true that the divine act whereby Jesus passed from his earthly life to his glorified existence did not occur in our time continuum, yet, it *corresponded* to our time continuum and in that sense can be dated as having occurred in the 30's A.D. And, in regard to the question of space, or place, the starting point of the transition of Jesus from his earthly to his glorified state was the historical (dead) Jesus who was located in a Jerusalem tomb. Thus, in a restricted sense at least, we can say that the resurrection occurred in space.[14]

Summary

We can attempt to synthesize this chapter. Marxsen claims that 20th century Christians can go back histori-

---

13. Art. cit., p. 386.
14. Lastly, if it is true, as is often held by Catholic and Protestant biblical scholars, that the postresurrection Christ founded the Church, then, according to O'Collins' opinion, it was not the historical Christ who founded the Church, nor did he found it in (our) time or space! He founded it outside of our world of time and space; he founded it in a "spiritual" time-space continuum. Would this be an issue of only terminology or of doctrine?

cally only to the point that the witnesses *claimed* they saw the risen Christ. Moreover, the divine act whereby Christ resurrected is known only through faith and not through history, even though (I add this, not Marxsen) the effect of this act, the appearances of Christ, may in a sense be called "historical."

X

Is Jesus Christ God?

The fundamental truth of Christianity is the divinity of Jesus. Though the meaning of this concept has been reconsidered periodically in the history of Christianity, the basic truth has gone, for the most part, undisputed since it was defined by the Council of Nicea in 325 A.D. Yet today many Christians are casually calling this truth into question, apparently unaware of the consequences of denying it. For if this central belief is denied, the bottom is knocked out of very many important teachings of the Christian faith. Some of the teachings that would have to be reconsidered are the doctrine of the Trinity, the meaning of the Eucharist, the efficacy of the sacrament of penance, the very authority of Jesus' teachings themselves. Likewise many cherished, though less essential, ideas in Christianity lose their power over men's minds if Jesus is merely a human "savior" rather than divine.

For example, it is a very consoling thought that God loved men enough to send his own son for their salvation. If Jesus is not uniquely God's son and of his substance, this love becomes somewhat diluted. If Jesus is only a human savior, his teachings lose some of their binding power over men's moral lives. The originality and authority of the Christian faith becomes practically no more than that of the Old Testament religion taught by the prophets sent by God.

It should be clear, then, that a Christian cannot lightly deny the divinity of Jesus, for doing so puts the entire faith of Christianity in a precarious situation. However, the objection may be raised at this point that we are already presupposing that which this chapter intends to discuss, namely the divinity of Jesus. This is an objection well raised, and it must be admitted that no one can "prove" the divinity of Jesus scientifically through historical, logical, psychological or any other kinds of arguments. The New Testament authors themselves did not write *in order to prove this,* much as they may have believed it. However, when one approaches any piece of literature with an unprejudiced mind, he must consider what theory best enables him to interpret the literature with inner consistency. In interpreting the New Testament, this basic theory must consider the possibility of the existence of the "supernatural." If one presupposes that the supernatural cannot exist, then he must find a way to explain the events of the New Testament in a manner consistent with his presupposition. Though many have tried to do this, it is a difficult task and leads to many problems and contradictions. For example, it becomes most difficult to explain the very origin and perdurance of Christianity, considering its more than humble beginnings with a group of ignorant and illiterate fishermen. However, if the reader is willing to concede the possibility of the supernatural, it becomes easier to interpret and explain the events of the New Testament. In relation to the example above, if one can agree to the possibility of divine "intervention" in the founding of Christianity, its existence today makes much more sense.

However, if one cannot flatly deny the divinity of Jesus without endangering the foundations of the Christian faith, one can certainly question the *meaning* of this traditional belief of Christians. It is certainly time for rethinking this idea in terms of modern categories, rather than the ancient Greek terms in which this doctrine was originally defined at Nicea. Irrelevance seems to be the most frequently raised objection to Christian teachings today and this objection can certainly apply to the traditional understanding of the divinity of Jesus. To many modern Christians, steeped as they are in the attitude of humanism, the humanity of Jesus is far more meaningful than his divinity. Some radical theologians think that they are paying Jesus the supreme compliment when they describe him as "the uniquely free man," or "the man for others." Jesus as a man who thoroughly feels for the plight of humans is more appealing and relevant to modern youth than Jesus as God with all the prerogatives of the divinity. They prefer to view Jesus as a model of one who has realized all the potentialities of a human being. (This preference is partly due to the influence of Teilhard de Chardin.)

The Problems Raised by the New Testament

In considering the fact or meaning of Jesus' divinity, we must first examine the New Testament texts traditionally used in support of this doctrine. The first group of texts to be considered relate to the question as to whether Jesus *himself* claimed to be divine. As a general answer to this question, it must be pointed out that Jesus never claimed to be divine in words expressly and indisputably said by him, such as "I am God." If Jesus in his lifetime *had* said that he was "God," he would have been misunderstood to mean that he was God in the sense of the Father because this was what "God" meant to his Jewish audience.

There are a number of Gospel statements attributed to Jesus which are used in support of the argument that he *did* claim to be divine. One example is the series of statements in the sermon on the mount which Jesus prefaced by "You have heard the commandment . . . but what *I* say to you is . . ." (Mt. 5:38-39). According to the interpretation usually given these sayings, Jesus is making himself superior to the ten commandments, the very heart of the Jewish moral law which was considered to have been given by God himself at Sinai.

In another place, Jesus seems to rank himself above the Old Testament prophets when he points to himself and says, "Behold, something greater than Jonah is here" (Mt. 12:41). Jesus is stronger than Satan whom Matthew calls "the strong Man" that Jesus "binds" (12:29), and the angels are conceived of as his servants when, after the temptation in the desert, they "came and ministered to him" (Mt. 4:11). Even his teachings are more lasting than the universe: "Heaven and earth will pass away, but my words will not pass away" (Mt. 24:35).

The five examples cited above are not cogent enough to prove that Jesus claimed to be divine. In these claims of superiority of his person or of his teachings over the ten commandments, the Old Testament prophets, Satan, the angels and the universe, it does not follow that he thereby claimed divinity but only that he had a very intimate relationship with God.

There are several texts which are more explicit than those cited above. One of the most striking statements used in support of the argument that Jesus claimed to be divine is found in Mark 2:10, where he is reported to have said to the paralytic, "That you may know that the Son of Man has authority on earth to forgive sins" (he said to the paralyzed man), "I command you: Stand up. Pick up your mat and go home." This statement loses its force if the form-critical scholars are correct in saying that these words were attributed to Christ *after Easter* since only then did the disciples know that Christ could forgive sins personally; in other words, Christ never said this even after Easter but the disciples attributed this power to him then and so the evangelist puts these words on his lips. Other scholars say that the story is written to defend the prevailing power of the Church at the time of the writing, which power to forgive sins was denied by the contemporary Jews.

Perhaps the most explicit texts wherein Jesus speaks of himself as "the Son" of God in the synoptic narratives of the public ministry is the following: "No one knows the son except the Father, and no one knows the Father except the son and anyone to whom the Son chooses to reveal him." (Mt. 11:27; Luke 10:22). According to J. Jeremias, an expert whose specialty is to translate the Greek back into the Aramaic language spoken by Jesus, it is possible that "the Son" is said as a parable or in parabolic style like "the sower went out to sow his seed."

In all of the above texts, the special relationship to the Father which Jesus indicates could be shared by other men and as such would not make him uniquely God's Son. None of these sayings, taken together or individually, proves that Jesus is divine or even that he claimed to be, whether he himself said them or whether they were merely attributed to him by the evangelists. They do, however, show his claim to an authority greater than any rabbi or prophet enjoyed.[1]

Do the Miracles of Jesus Reveal His Divinity?

We will now consider whether the miracles of Jesus are a support to the argument that he was divine. In the former apologetics, the miracles of Jesus were given as indisputable "proof" of his divinity. While not denying the apologetic value of Jesus' miracles, modern studies show that the principal purpose of the miracles of Jesus as described in the synoptic gospels was to announce the arrival of the Messiah and his kingdom. The highest expression of faith which Jesus ever asked after performing a miracle was an affirmation of him as the Messiah. Hence the belief he was asking for was open-ended.

Besides proclaiming through his miracles, the arrival

---

1. Statements of Jesus found in John's Gospel have been omitted from the above discussion because it is more difficult to distinguish in John than in the first three Gospels, which are actually the words of Jesus and which are the words of John attributed to him. For example, "I and the Father are one" (10:30) was often understood to signify a claim for divinity because the following verse 33 reads "not for a good work do we stone you, but for blasphemy, because you, being a man, make yourself *God*."

of his kingdom, Jesus also performed his miracles in fulfillment of Old Testament prophecies. He told the disciples of John the Baptist that the arrival of his kingdom is manifested by his miracles of healing the sick and raising the dead to life. For example, it is widely held that in response to questions of who he is, Christ points to his works as a fulfillment of various Messianic prophecies in Isaiah, which depict the Messiah as a suffering servant. One thinks immediately of Matthew who narrates that the disciples of John the Baptist asked Christ "Are you he who is to come?" and Jesus answers: "Go and report to John what you have heard and seen: the blind see, the lame walk, the lepers are cleansed, the deaf hear, the dead rise, the poor have the gospel preached to them." (11:4-5).

Turning to John's gospel it becomes clear that John does not present the miracles of Christ as an announcement of the arrival of his kingdom but only as acts belonging to the ministry of Jesus and as an illustration of God's power. But this is still different from saying that the miracles were primarily meant to prove Christ's divinity.

Do the New Testament Writers Claim Jesus Is Divine?

Do the evangelists claim that Jesus is divine through any of the episodes of his life?

There is hardly an episode which clearly aims at proclaiming Jesus' divinity. The two episodes that come close to this purpose are those of Jesus' baptism and transfiguration. But very few outstanding scholars, if any, see these scenes as claiming Jesus' divinity. Those that do appeal to the voice of God the father from heaven saying: "This is my beloved *son,* in whom I am well pleased" (Mt. 3:17). But it is not obvious that the words "my beloved son" signify exclusively the one *divine* son of God, Jesus.

The Divinity of Jesus Proclaimed by His Titles

If the belief in Jesus as divine does not arise from his own claims or his miracles, from what does it arise? The strongest expressions of belief in the divinity of Jesus are the titles by which the early Christians called him after his resurrection, when the full impact of his identity came home to them.

The first or earliest title which the Christians used to signify the divinity of Jesus was the title "Lord." This usage was based on Psalm 110, verse 1: "The Lord said to my lord, sit at my right hand." This expressed the belief in Jesus as risen and seated at the right hand of God (cf. Acts 2:33; Rom. 8:32). Note that it was the title "Lord" rather than "son of God" which the Christians first used to designate Jesus as divine. Another title which the early Christians associated with Christ's divinity was "the judge of the living and the dead" (Acts 10:42).

The title "Savior" when said of Jesus in the New Testament expresses the belief in God himself saving men: "God exalted him at his right hand as leader and *Savior,* to give repentance to Israel and forgiveness of sins" (Acts 5:32). In the epistles to Timothy and Titus the Greek word for Savior, *soter,* is said of both God the Father and Jesus without any change of meaning.

One of the most mysterious titles expressing Jesus' divinity is the expression "I AM." In John's Gospel there are eight passages in which the designation of himself by this expression is attributed to Jesus (e.g. Jn. 8:58; 12:26;

17:24). This statement is a direct and deliberate reference to God's way of identifying himself to Moses in Exodus 3:13-14. In John 8:58, Jesus' audience recognizes this allusion so unmistakably that they attempt to stone him, stoning being the penalty for blasphemy.

Theos, the Greek word for God, is applied directly to Jesus three times in the New Testament. The first is the expression of faith made by Thomas after the resurrection. After having doubted the word of the other apostles who claimed to have seen Jesus risen, Thomas himself sees Jesus and exclaims: "My Lord and my God (*theos*)!" (Jn. 20:28). This is the first explicitly recorded act of faith in the divinity of the *resurrected* Christ. Even R. Bultmann admits that this is a powerful example of belief in Jesus' divinity for he holds it as the only one in the New Testament. The second use of *theos* in reference to Jesus is in John's prologue (1:1): "In the beginning was the Word; and the Word was in God's presence, and the Word was *God* (*theos*)." The third use of *theos* is the statement: "Your throne, O God is forever and ever" which is said of Jesus in Heb. 1:8-9 and taken from Ps. 44:7-8 where it was said in reference to a Hebrew monarch. Thus the author of the epistle to the Hebrews expresses his faith in the divinity of Jesus.

Conclusions

These titles were absent from the accounts of the earthly ministry of Jesus. They speak of Jesus *after* his resurrection. (This is not true of the title "Lord" by which Jesus was called during his ministry. However, "Lord" as used then simply meant "master.") Therefore these titles cannot be adduced as "proofs" of the divinity of Jesus, but rather they show that after his resurrection the early Christians *believed* Jesus to be the divine son of God.

What did "divinity" mean to the authors of the New Testament? The term itself, "divinity," is Greek rather than Semitic. The titles bestowed on Jesus discussed above give a penetrating insight on the early Christian concept of Jesus' divinity. The title "Lord" (*Kurios* in Greek) recalled to the minds of the early Christians the Yahweh of the Old Testament who was "judge" and "savior" of all men. In other words, to the early Christians Jesus' divinity consisted in sharing the qualities and privileges of the Old Testament Yahweh. The use of "I AM" and *"theos"* support this view. Only after New Testament times was the belief in Jesus' divinity understood and formulated in the Greek concepts by which Catholic teaching has always explained this mystery: two natures, human and divine, in one person of the Word.

The titles by which Jesus was called are functional—that is, they signify the roles of Lord, judge, savior, *theos* which Jesus plays in regard to men—rather than explicitly saying something about what Jesus is in himself in his "nature."

It seems reasonable to conclude, then, that Jesus himself did not claim to be divine either through explicit statements or indirectly through his miracles. The New Testament authors assert their belief in the divinity of Jesus through their use of certain titles by which to designate him after his resurrection. For many present-day Christians, the belief of the New Testament writers is sufficient authority for the doctrine of Jesus as divine, because these Christians have *faith*—that there is only one author of the Bible, the Holy Spirit, under whose inspiration the New Testament authors wrote. Hence, the

New Testament writers under the influence of the Holy Spirit would be authentically interpreting the teaching of Jesus about himself, namely, that he is divine.

For some Protestant biblical scholars, for example, R. Bultmann and his school and other Christians, however, there is a vast difference—from the point of view of authority and doctrine—between Jesus explicitly making a statement and the New Testament writers making a statement about Jesus. For these people, only the indisputable sayings of Jesus are authoritative; the interpretations and beliefs of the New Testament authors are fallible. Therefore, if Jesus himself never made the claim to divinity, it is not necessary for Christians to conclude to the fact of his divinity.

New Insight from Dogmatic Theology

Until now we have considered the problem of Jesus' divinity from the viewpoint of scriptural data. New developments in systematic theology shed light on the problem from the point of view of the consideration of Jesus' knowledge or awareness of his identity as the divine Son of God. In other words, the question being asked is "If Jesus was divine, was he *conscious* of that fact throughout his life?" We will consider the insights of several contemporary Roman Catholic theologians on this question.

Riedlinger

The most substantial new Catholic work on Christology is by H. Riedlinger.[2] Riedlinger does not hold the tradi-

---

2. Riedlinger, H., *Geschichtlichkeit und Vollendung des Wissens Christi,* Freiburg, 1966.

tional view of Jesus' knowledge: that Jesus enjoyed the beatific vision (the Heavenly vision) of God from the first moment of his human existence and that in addition to his acquired knowledge through human experience, he received infused knowledge from God. Riedlinger describes Jesus' knowledge as the "historical vision of God." "Vision of God" means that Jesus was aware of his divinity; while "historical" alludes to the biblical report of Jesus, for example, his limited knowledge (Mark 13:32) and progress of understanding of himself and the world (Luke 2:52). He concludes with a realistic note: "We can never determine with absolute clarity and distinctness the actual levels, processes and limits of Jesus' knowledge" (p. 156).

Hulsbosch

A. Hulsbosch attracted attention in explaining Jesus' unity of two natures in relation to an evolutionary theory. In his view, in each successive evolutionary phase there are realized the possibilities latent in the preceding phases, rather than the addition to each phase of an entirely new principle. Thus man is not matter with spirit added, but is rather spiritual (sic) matter, at least in part. Hulsbosch applies this concept to the identity of Jesus as follows: "In Christ there is not the presence of a man in which a presence of God different from this asserts itself; no, this presence is as much the presence of God. Christ is perfectly one because he is only man but as such he is precisely the manifestation of God."[3] Hulsbosch adds:

3. *Tijschrift voor Theologie,* Vol. 6, p. 257, 1966. See *Herder Correspondence,* vol. 4, p. 220, 1967.

"Christ's preexistence as divine is nothing other than 'the retroprojection of the subjectivity of the man Jesus as Son of God.' "[4] Hulsbosch has found a relevant tool for theological explanation in the concepts and language of evolution but he does not preserve the doctrine of traditional faith. In spite of his intentions, to say that Christ is "only man" even if he is somehow "the manifestation of God," his statement is in fact a denial of Jesus' uniqueness as "Son of God."

B. Lonergan[5]

An illuminating insight on the problem of Christ's consciousness of his divinity comes from B. Lonergan, S.J. He distinguishes between consciousness, a knowledge that is suppressed, and on the other hand an objective knowledge, a knowledge composed of clearly formulated judgments. Our Graeco-Scholastic background disposes us to presume that objective knowledge makes for a perfect human being but "in attributing a certain ignorance to Christ we are not in fact implying that he in any way fell short of human perfection; on the contrary, were he omniscient he could not be perfectly human." (The most eloquent example of Christ's ignorance is found in Mark 13:32: "But of that day or that hour no one knows, not even the angels in heaven, *nor the Son,* but only the Father." He was speaking of the end of the world, most probably.) Accordingly, Christ was conscious at least in

---

4. *Tijschrift voor Theologie,* Vol. 6, p. 266, 1966.
5. For the rest of this chapter I am indebted to J. Ashton, S.J. "Theological Trends: The Consciousness of Christ I," *The Way,* vol. 10 (no. 1, January, 1970), pp. 59-71.

a nonreflective way, of his own Person of the divine Word, his divine personality.

A Tentative Solution

Karl Rahner suggests that Jesus at the beginning of his life on earth had a nonreflective consciousness of his own divinity and this developed into a more explicit knowledge. Let us consider this possibility in relation to the problem: As God, Jesus must know all things; as man, his knowledge must be limited. In becoming man, Jesus temporarily—in the world of time—divested himself of all his divine prerogatives. This means that he exercised his divine will in a renunciation of the privileges and qualities of his divine nature. Thus we can say that he was subject to ignorance and doubt and uncertainty and that he never attained a clear objective knowledge of his own divinity though he was conscious of it nonreflectively.

A Final Word

In conclusion, we may say that from K. Rahner and B. Lonergan Catholics can hold that Christ also suffered from ignorance and doubt, uncertainty and fear (e.g., the agony in the garden and the cry from the cross) and that he never attained a clear objective knowledge of his own divinity though he was conscious of it nonreflectively.

This recent tentative solution helps us to understand how Christ was like men in everything except sin. This solution enables us to penetrate the words of the epistle to the Hebrews, 2:17: "It was imperative that he should be made like his brothers *in every respect,* and might we add, "even in doubt and ignorance"?